Fencing With the Smallsword

Michael J. Stevens

Foreword by Predrag Agatonović

Fencing
With the Smallsword

The Art of Swordsmanship for the Beginner

Meyer & Meyer Sport

British Library Cataloguing in Publication Data
A catalogue record for this book is available from the British Library

Fencing With the Smallsword
Maidenhead: Meyer & Meyer Sport (UK) Ltd., 2026
ISBN: 978-1-78255-287-1

Aachen, Auckland, Beirut, Cairo, Cape Town, Dubai, Hägendorf, Hong Kong, Indianapolis, Maidenhead, Manila, New Delhi, Singapore, Sydney, Tehran, Vienna

Member of the World Sport Publishers' Association (WSPA), www.w-s-p-a.org

Printed by King Printing Company, Inc., Lowell, MA
www.kingprinting.com
Printed in the United States of America

ISBN 978-1-78255-287-1
Email: info@m-m-sports.com
www.thesportspublisher.com

Manufacturer under the GPSR
Meyer & Meyer Fachverlag und Buchhandel GmbH
Von-Coels-Str. 390
52080 Aachen, Germany
www.dersportverlag.de

Contents

Foreword

The smallsword, that elegant paragon of duelling finesse, was not merely a weapon but a statement - a delightful blend of practicality and style that had enchanted both the battlefield and ballroom alike. With its fast slender blade and refined hilt, it embodied the notion that one does not need brute force to command respect. Instead, it championed the art of precision and grace, making it the ideal companion for a quick flourish in an argument or a sharp witty response. Whether one was defending their honour or simply fending off an unwanted suitor, the smallsword allowed for an expressiveness that larger weapons simply could not match, proving that sometimes, less really is more.

It is my great pleasure to see that the spirit of this elegant weapon still lives, and this book is a great place for aspiring swordsmen and swordswomen. This book is a valuable resource for anyone looking to master the art of swordsmanship, offering a comprehensive guide to both technique and etiquette. It provides clear, step-by-step instructions on the essential movements and stances, ensuring that novices can quickly gain confidence in their skills. For anyone wishing to start navigating the complexities of swordplay with equal finesse, this book proves to be an indispensable guide.

—Predrag Agatonović
President of FEATHER - School of Historical Fencing
CEO of FEATHER SMALLSWORDS

Acknowledgements

I am delighted that historical fencing expert **Predrag Agatonović** was willing to write the foreword, and I'm most grateful for his endorsement of this text. I share his enthusiasm for the smallsword, and I have practised all the exercises included here using a FEATHER smallsword that he made.

I would also like to thank

- **Alan Wolsoncroft** for traditional fencing instruction spanning several decades. Without this background, I would not have had the knowledge to write this book. I have included an exercise he devised for practising the *remise*.
- **Nicholas Stephenson** and **Colin Woods** for featuring in the photographs.
- **Colin Woods** for the author and hand position photographs.

Preface

Having been enthralled by sword fights I had seen in films, I was excited to discover that fencing was available as a sporting option on a Wednesday afternoon when, back in 1967, I enrolled on a science course at the local technical college, so I joined the class straight away. A little later I started attending an evening class in fencing where we were taught by Alan Wolsoncroft, a British Academy of Fencing instructor, who had learned his teaching skills from Bob Anderson, the former national coach who later arranged many fight sequences for films.

Starting with the foil, we spent the first year learning the thrusts and parries in class lessons, and after that we were allowed to fence against each other. I, and some of my sparring partners, passed the Amateur Fencing Association's bronze and silver foil proficiency tests and, as time went by, we did the same with the épée and sabre.

In 1996, the local council axed the evening classes and we formed our own club, Salle Poisson d'Or, so we could continue to fence on a regular basis. The name of the club alludes to the fact that Alan often complained we had the memories of goldfish when it came to remembering what he taught us! While some fencers were interested in competing, others, myself included, simply enjoyed fencing each other at the club. After a while, Salle Poisson d'Or merged with the Ranmore fencing club but retained its name. The club prospered until the Covid-19 outbreak in 2020, when we reluctantly disbanded it due to diminishing numbers and the fact that Alan, now in his mid-80s, wanted to retire from teaching.

Not wishing to give up fencing, I went along to another local club that seemed to be thriving. Here, I was not only the oldest fencer but also the only one who could fence with all three weapons. When it came to foil, one of the coaches informed me that I was practising *classical fencing*, which I had never heard of, and he said they didn't teach it like that anymore (I had already worked that out). Even my traditional hold on the French grip was viewed as an oddity: the few who were using French grips were taught to hold them near the pommel. With my traditional training, I saw their efforts as uncontrolled and imprecise, and it was hard to picture where the moves they were making might appear as recommendations in any fencing manual. Their sword arms were not being straightened at the onset of attacks, which explained why nobody was attempting compound attacks. Counter-parries were seen extremely rarely, and one of the coaches didn't even know what a counter-parry was. In spite of all this, the club members were progressing through their proficiency tests and doing well in competitions, which is clearly the main objective of a modern sports fencing club.

When attacking, a straight arm, with the hand raised above the shoulder, is advisable because it keeps the body at a safe distance and keeps one guarded against the opponent's lethal point – it is plain good swordsmanship and was recommended by all the old masters. Originally, the rules for competitions were devised to encourage good swordsmanship. The attacker was defined as the first fencer to straighten the sword arm with the point threatening the target, and this fencer would be awarded a point in the event of both parties hitting at the same time, as the opponent must have made a reckless move instead of defending himself. Now, however, the rules are not being interpreted in the old way, and other movements made by a fencer may be considered to identify him as the attacker. Very likely this change happened because so many fencers were turning up at competitions without having the knowledge or the discipline to fence properly – nobody was straightening the sword arm when attacking, which meant that in the event of a double hit, both hits would have to be annulled, as it would be impossible to identify an attacker. These days it is not unusual for the referee to consult a video play-back to determine which fencer had right of way and could be awarded a point – the crazy thing being that, in a real sword fight, both swordsmen would be injured or dead.

A good swordsman will use a simple parry to deflect the attacking blade so that it clears his body by a few inches. This is no longer being taught to foilists because of the way the rules are now interpreted. The rules say that right of way passes to the defender once a parry has been taken, but often not much more than a contact of blades is deemed acceptable as a parry, so incomplete parries have become the norm and the defender is at risk of being hit even though his riposte will be given priority.

Getting in close and jabbing to and fro with the sword arm is sometimes seen. This is very bad fencing, but it has been around for a long time. Alfred Hutton in his book *The Swordsman*, published in the late nineteenth century, writes:

> **... a stabbing stroke like that of a poniard is a vicious habit to which some people are much addicted, and one which any student of fence, who desires to achieve a reputation as a swordsman, must scrupulously avoid ... it is in reality the last resource of a hopelessly bad swordsman to score a hit which he is unable to effect by more legitimate means. There is but one sensible way of treating a man who persists in using this style of attack, and that is to refuse flatly to fence with him at all.**

It seems to me that modern competitive fencing has drifted too far from its duelling origins. It has morphed into a game aimed at maximising the points scored while taking into account the way the rules are interpreted. That doesn't really matter to those who are only interested in who can score the most points, but it does to anyone who is interested in the art of fencing itself. One major contributor to this state of affairs has been the introduction of electric scoring equipment that can separate hits that arrive as close as one twenty-fifth of a second apart. This has encouraged fencers to become more athletic so they can use speed and agility to land a hit fractionally before they get hit themselves, which is not something any sane duellist would try to do. Fencers are now referred to as athletes - athletics has replaced swordplay and the art of fencing is getting lost.

Another issue with electric scoring, particularly with foil, is that a hit can be scored with a very light touch that would not be enough to stop a sword fight. Before the use of electric equipment, hits had to have 'character of penetration' - there had to be at least a slight bend in the blade, making it appear that, had it been sharp, it would have penetrated about three inches.

There is a difference between being a good fighter and a good fencer. Some people who are good at scoring hits are not actually very good fencers. They often have a limited repertoire of actions at their disposal, and those they do use are executed badly. Those who can score the hits are always lauded as being good fencers, but in my view, fencing is about what goes on between the hits, and the best fencers are those who manage to keep a sequence of thrusts and parries going for some time before a hit is scored to spoil the fun. Modern sports fencing favours the fighter rather than the fencer. Training to score the most hits, taking into account the way the rules are interpreted, is now quite different from training to stay uninjured in a sword fight.

Sports fencing weapons all differ in some respects from the real swords they are derived from. No sword ever had the orthopaedic or pistol grip, which is now ubiquitous but was originally designed for people with weak wrists. The foil was originally a practice weapon for the smallsword, but modern foils are longer and some blades are springy enough to flick and deliver a hit on the opponent's back. This would not be possible with real swords, as they are just not that flexible.

The épée is a development of the *épée de combat*, the latest duelling sword, but this didn't have a large offset guard and it was used at a time when duels were being fought for first blood – body hits were deliberately avoided because the consequences of seriously wounding or killing an opponent were too dire.

In the early days of sabre fencing, the legs were a valid target – obviously they had to be well padded. When fighting with real sabres, cutting through the hamstrings was a favourite ploy, as it put the opponent out of action straight away. For reasons of safety, the sabre now has an unrealistically thin and extremely manoeuvrable blade, so it doesn't handle anything like a real sabre, and now that electric scoring equipment is used, touches with the flat of the blade also count as valid hits.

While I was pondering the demise of the art of swordsmanship, I discovered that Historical European Martial Arts (HEMA) clubs were using smallswords in a way that more closely resembled the duelling situation, and I was hooked on this weapon. Initial attempts at smallsword fencing turned out more like brawling in a pub car park, but after studying some of the available books on the subject and practising the lessons described therein, it started to look more civilised. It was a welcome antidote to sports fencing, and it was a lot of fun.

This book began when I transcribed exercises that I found in the old (French school) manuals for myself and my sparring partners to practise. Much to my surprise, many of these were very similar to the exercises that Alan used to have us run through in class lessons when I first learned to fence. I gradually expanded the accompanying text to a point where I thought others might be interested in reading it. I hope it will prove useful to those starting out with the smallsword.

Introduction

Unfortunately, HEMA clubs, where one might be able to practise smallsword fencing, are few and far between, and the smallsword is not usually their favourite weapon. This makes it rather difficult to learn to fence with this fascinating weapon. Since it is closely related to foil fencing, a good way to start is to learn the foil at a sports fencing club, and then read up on the smallsword and start practising what you've read whenever you get the chance. I think the smallsword is an excellent second weapon to master after the foil.

Here, I present a practical guide to learning to fence with the smallsword for sports fencers who want to try this weapon. The most important part is a set of comprehensive exercises taken mainly from old manuals of French-style fencing. These are written up in a concise form, using modern fencing terminology, and all the terms used are explained in a previous chapter on fencing theory. In the following chapter I have constructed some example fight sequences. It is a good idea to practise these before venturing on to free play, as they will give you some idea of what fencing with the smallsword should be like. After that there are some exercises to try with the eyes closed in order to develop a good feel through the blade.

Note that I have written throughout for the right-handed fencer. Left-handers will need to interpret the text to suit them and swap left and right where appropriate.

Unlike sports fencing, where the emphasis has shifted over the last century from swordplay to athletics, here the swordplay remains all important. Sports clubs like to run, sometimes lengthy, warm-up sessions before the fencers get to handle a weapon, and after that not much, if any, time is spent on blade-work. Here you can have a sword in your hand right from the start because working through the exercises or the fight sequences is a much more interesting way to warm up. Smallsword fencing should be thought of as a martial art, not as a sport. It will appeal more to those who enjoy learning to master the intricacies of swordplay than to those who just take pleasure in scoring hits.

There have been no significant changes in the way fencing has been taught right from the introduction of the smallsword, almost up to the present day. Anyone who has been taught foil fencing, particularly in the classical manner, will have no difficulty in transitioning to the smallsword. Those who have merely been taught the rudiments before being allowed to fight, and who concentrate exclusively on instinctive movements, will have more work to do if they want to get the best out of this weapon.

Some smallsword users are interested in consulting the old manuals and recreating exactly what was done in the past. I see the smallsword as a perfectly respectable modern fencing weapon, and I'm not interested in just copying the past for the sake of it. Fencing has evolved, and some actions that were practised by the ancients were later discarded or superseded by others that proved more effective. I have included some of the older actions where practice has proved that they can still be effective, but not others, such as the *volte* and the rapier fencer's *acrobatic lunge*. I have deliberately omitted various disarming techniques discussed in the earlier manuals involving grabbing the opponent's wrist or arm, as they are likely to cause injury in a recreational setting, and also because they were rejected as far back as 1780 by John McArthur, as he considered them unsafe. I would not suggest reviving the elaborate salute sequences that were fashionable in the past, and I have not described them here. I have not included exercises for an obsolete thrust known as the *flanconade* because it is inferior to the *croisé* or the *bind*, both of which could be better used in its place.

I have retained the guards and parries with the sword hand in pronation (palm down) where they were written that way in the old manuals. It is generally accepted now that positions with the hand in supination (palm up) or semi-supination are superior, but what works best in competitive fencing isn't necessarily best in smallsword fencing. While I would not discourage anyone from using supination in preference to pronation, I would encourage fencers to practise prime, seconde and tierce: they are easy to manage with the more extended arm of the smallsword user and they add variety, making for more interesting fencing. The change from sixte or tierce to seconde can be effected very rapidly by a twist of the forearm, and prime is very easy to adopt starting from tierce.

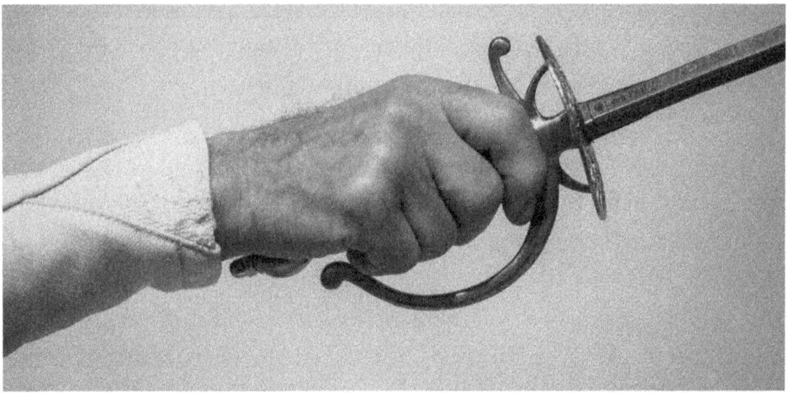

Hand in pronation.

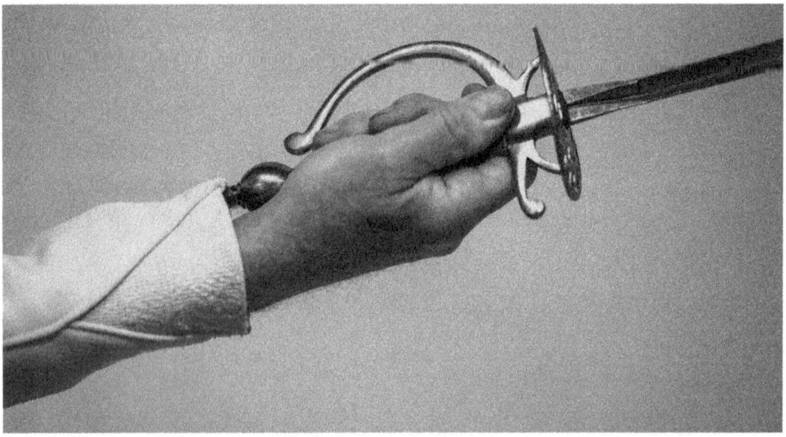

Hand in supination.

The old manuals all make much use of the *appel*, which is a stamping of the leading foot on the floor. I have not included this in the exercises or fight sequences, as I've found it has no noticeable effect. Another suggestion in one of the old manuals is to shudder the shoulders to frighten the opponent. Maybe the French are more easily intimidated than we are! Yet another trait from former times, which has now fallen into disuse, is to beat the opponent's blade when parrying.

A number of features of smallsword fencing make it more like the real thing than modern competitive sports fencing:

- The smallsword itself is modelled on real swords that were used back in the day. In particular, the pistol grip, which is now popular in sports fencing, is not allowed.
- Fencers are not restricted to a piste.
- A glove is needed on the left hand because it can be used to parry, to deflect a blade after parrying or to grab the opponent's blade. Note, however, that very little use of the left hand is described in the early manuals and, while grabbing a foil was considered acceptable, grabbing a sword in a duel was not recommended.
- It is acceptable to move the sword to the other hand while fencing, though most fencers will not want to do it, and it will not be practicable when using a sword knot or a martingale as a restraining device.
- When scoring, the usual convention is that if both fencers receive a hit in the same period of fencing time, it counts as a double hit and penalises both of them, even if one hit arrives before the other.
- While a few experiments with electric scoring have been made, in general, the weapon has not been electrified and fencers acknowledge hits received.

This guide to smallsword fencing will, I hope, encourage others to take it up. It provides all the information needed to get started. If you like the idea of trying some swashbuckling, I can thoroughly recommend studying the smallsword.

Chapter 1

The Smallsword

The French and the Dutch were mainly responsible for the introduction of the smallsword, which started to appear around the middle of the seventeenth century and was popular throughout the eighteenth century. Being shorter, lighter and less cumbersome than the earlier rapier, it was not only more convenient to carry about on one's person but it was also considerably faster and more manoeuvrable in hand, allowing for compound attacks and parries in quick succession. It was ideal for self-defence and popular for duelling. A few smallswords had sharp edges, but the vast majority did not. Essentially, they were thrusting weapons only, and this is the case with smallsword fencing - only hits with the point are allowed.

Take-up of this new weapon in early 18th century England was rather slow due to a natural English dislike of anything French, but royalty and the nobility started to carry smallswords, and before long they became fashion accessories and status symbols for the gentry too. Fencing academies were set up, for example by Domenico Angelo and Jean Olivier in Soho and Fleet Street, respectively, in London, where students could learn to fence in the French manner. Foils were used in these establishments, but the early ones were shorter than those we use today, both in the length of the blade and the grip. Contemporary engravings depict fencers in their everyday clothes without masks - which were not invented until around the middle of the eighteenth century. Apparently, it was not uncommon for fencing masters to lose an eye! Initially, fencing academies focused on combat - giving fencers the best chance of defending their lives should the need arise. Gradually there was a change of emphasis towards fencing as a recreational activity:

sports fencing had arrived. From early on, women as well as men were accepted as members of fencing academies and, occasionally, women were involved in duels too.

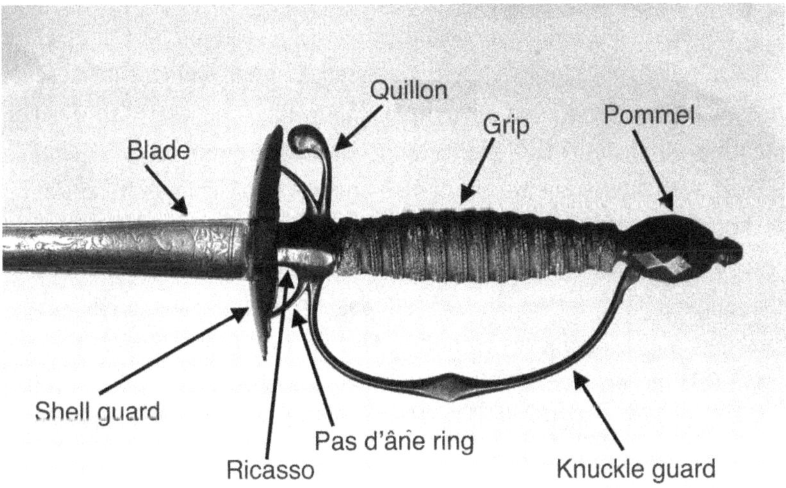

A smallsword from the Regency period in the author's collection.

There appears to be no universally agreed set of material rules for the construction of sports smallswords for fencing. Orthopaedic/pistol grips are not allowed. One set of tournament rules states that

Hilts must be of the French, Spanish or Italian type and must be constructed in as historically accurate a manner as possible within the limits of safety. The hilts of weapons must be constructed without any type of eccentricity with regard to the quillons, knuckle guard or ricasso, and without anachronism, such as offset guards. The guard of the weapon can be no wider than 4.5 inches and the quillons must not protrude more than one inch beyond the circumference of the guard. Blades must be standard épée or double-width épée, with a length in the range of 29-35 inches.

Note that double width 'musketeer' blades are heavier and stiffer than épée blades. They can still be used with sports fencing clothing but they will hurt and mark more – chest protectors and well-padded gloves are advisable.

The average blade length for smallswords was held to be 32 inches. Data from a collection of 26 weapons classified as smallswords in a museum revealed blade lengths ranging from 28 to 35 inches, with an average length of 31 inches. Their weights ranged from 252 g (8.9 oz) to 535 g (1 lb 2.9 oz), with an average weight of 407.4 g (14.4 oz). The English translation of Angelo's book states that the total length of the sword from pommel to point should not exceed 38 inches. This is a translation error. Checking the original French text, it says 38 pouces. The translator has simply changed pouces to inches without adjusting the measurement. A pouce was 1.066 inches, making 38 pouces equal to 40.508 inches. With a typical hilt length of 6.5 inches, Angelo's recommended maximum blade length would be 34 inches. Taller people would buy longer blades. One guideline for selecting the correct length was that with the point resting on the floor, the pommel should be level with the hip. Intuitively it would seem to be an advantage to have a longer blade but this is not the case, as it can be more unwieldy and less useful if fighting at close quarters when it may be necessary to withdraw the arm to disengage.

Some clubs use number 5 épée blades, but these are longer than the average length of a smallsword. (Adding 30 to the blade number gives roughly the length in inches.) Number 2 épée blades are easy to obtain, as they are popular with junior épéeists. These are much more suitable and widely used by smallsword fencers. A number 2 épée blade, fitted with a foil guard and an ambidextrous grip, makes a good smallsword training weapon, though the grip is longer than that of a real smallsword and the pommel can get in the way, particularly when the hand is in pronation because the handle extends beyond the wrist joint. Some blades are provided with a dummy electric point and some with a rubber button. The latter has the advantage that it will stick to the target more easily (as would the sharp point of a real sword), but it also more prone to catching on a blade attempting a cut-over.

It is a matter of personal preference whether a blade has a 'set' or not – that is, a slight bend at the shoulder in one direction or another. Antique smallswords in the main are dead straight. Angelo recommended a set towards quarte, which is the way many modern foils and épées are set. Personally, I like the blade to form a straight-line extension of my arm when I hold it out straight, without having to kink my wrist; a slight bend inwards from sixte brings that about.

Smallsword hilts are not easy to find. Many are rather expensive and some are quite weighty. Brass was used in the past but not on quality smallswords, and it is used on some fencing smallswords today but, being a denser alloy than steel, it can make them heavier. Brass is also softer than steel and likely to get marked more easily when in regular use. Hilts do need to be resilient – some antique smallswords have intricately decorated silver hilts, which were clearly not intended for combat, as silver is not sufficiently robust. Smallsword design evolved over the years that it was in vogue. Gradually the rings atrophied until they were no more than claws, and the shell diminished in size while the weapon remained part of a gentleman's dress code without any real expectation that the owner would need to use it in combat. The earlier designs give more protection to the hand, and these are a better choice for fencing, Continually attacking the opponent's sword hand does not lead to very interesting fencing, which is probably why, right from the start, foil fencers considered the arms to be off target, and why the large guards on sports épées were developed.

Most, but not all, smallswords had a knuckle guard, and a few examples had a chain in place of solid metal. Knuckle guards are not essential on fencing weapons, but if present, they need to be sturdy enough to cope with being knocked about. If the smallsword is likely to be used against cutting weapons rather than just other smallswords, then a knuckle guard is probably a good idea, but if you want the weapon to be ambidextrous, then a hilt without a knuckle guard will be more suitable and the blade should be dead straight.

Many antique smallsword grips had a beechwood core that was wrapped by a specialist with wire braiding. Some wire-wrapped grips are made today for fencing swords, but they are expensive. Leather-covered wooden grips are good to hold, while varnished wood can prove slippery in the hand. Grips with a round cross section are most common, presumably because they are quick and easy to produce by turning on a lathe. However, some fencers prefer a grip with a rectangular cross section. Anyone with DIY skills might like to try making their own instead of using those that are commercially available.

The part of the blade that is hidden inside the grip is known as the *tang*, a corruption of *tongue*, the name by which it was known in former times. Originally the tang was welded in place after the blade had been forged. The edge of the blade on the side of the knuckle guard is known as the true edge, and the other as the false edge. Many antique blades and all smallsword fencing blades are a V shape in cross section. They are mounted so that the swordsman's thumb is on the side of the groove, and this will be uppermost when in quarte. Parries in prime, seconde, tierce, quarte and septime are made with the true edge, while those in sixte and octave are made with the false edge. (The parries are explained in chapter 2, Some Fencing Theory.) The half of the blade nearest the hilt is known as the *forte*, and the half nearest the point as the *foible*, often translated as *feeble* in the older manuals.

Steam (non-electric) foils are fitted with martingales – loops of leather through which fingers are slipped so that, in the event of being disarmed, the weapon will not go flying off and injure someone. J. D. Aylward, in his book *The Small-Sword in England* reports that advertisements in newspapers

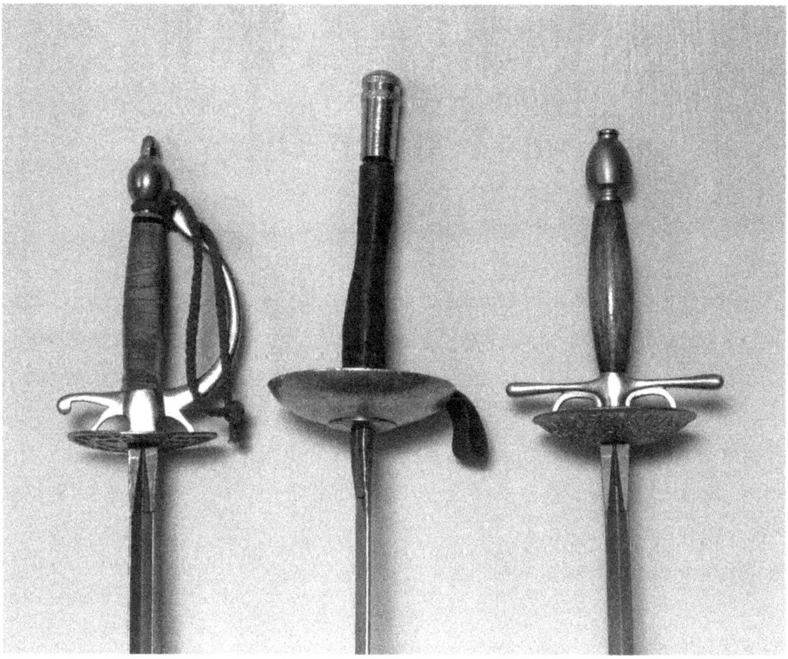

Example smallswords for fencing: 1. Hilt from Feather Smallswords, fitted with homemade oak grip bound with leather, and sword knot. 2. Foil hilt from Leon Paul with an ambidextrous grip and a martingale. 3. Hilt from Feather Smallswords with a varnished wooden grip. All fitted with Leon Paul No. 2 épée blades.

for lost swords included descriptions of sword knots. These were loops, for example of black ribbon, tied at the end of the knuckle guard near the pommel, through which the wrist could be slipped. Frederick Wilkinson, in his book *Edged Weapons*, notes that a French code for duelling stated that sword knots were permitted. They started to appear in the seventeenth century. Nobody seems to be using them now, but I can recommend them, as they make it easy to retrieve the sword if you are disarmed, and they are an obvious safety feature.

Chapter 2
Some Fencing Theory

The fencing exercises in the next chapter are written in a succinct form using standard terms from French fencing theory. It is apparent that many sports fencers these days are completing their training courses without learning any of the terminology. Some don't even know the names of the guard positions or the types of parry available. This chapter provides the information needed to understand the exercises. It is essential reading for the beginner or modern sports fencer, and a good refresher for those with a background in classical fencing.

The *flèche* and the *ballestra* are Italian moves that have been accepted in modern fencing, but they are not included here because they were not discussed in the old smallsword manuals.

2.1 Terminology

Fencing terminology has not been consistent through the ages. Domenico Angelo's (1763) *feather* parry is the same as *sixte*. What we know as a *septime* parry was called the *semicircle*, and *quinte* is the term both Girard (1740) and Angelo used for what we now call *octave*. Just to confuse matters further, John MacArthur claims that seconde was formerly known as *quinte*. He uses octave, which logically would have been coined after sixte and septime, but he doesn't use either of these terms! A thrust in sixte was known as a thrust *quarte over the arm*, and a thrust in *septime* was called a thrust in *low quarte*. Interestingly, a more recent 1890 publication *The Boy's Modern Playmate* still talks of *half-circle* rather than *septime*, and it too uses the expression *quarte over the arm*. It also likens an assault with foils to a smallsword fight, but this similarity has since been lost because of the way competitive foil fencing has evolved since that time.

The old manuals used the term *return of the wrist* to describe a thrust made by extending the arm but without lunging, so it covers renewed attacks, ripostes on the lunge and ripostes when the opponent is on the lunge. As this term in not now in general use, I have not grouped the exercises for this together under this heading.

Readers of the old manuals should be aware that I am using modern terminology in the descriptions of the smallsword exercises.

2.2 How to Hold the Smallsword

The classic hold of the French grip is recommended regardless of whether you are using a foil hilt or one fashioned after a real smallsword (see the following photo). With the latter, place your thumb on the side of the grip roughly where the rings cross the ricasso, or about 0.5–1 inch from the shell. Curl your index finger under on the opposite side and lay the remaining fingers flat on the grip. Some users prefer to straighten the forefinger and lay it alongside the quillon or knuckle guard. It is important not to put your fingers through the rings, assuming they are large enough to accommodate them, as there is a risk of getting them broken if you are disarmed. The pommel should rest on the inside of your wrist.

The old manuals talk of manipulating the weapon with the wrist, but it is easily light enough to be controlled with the fingers, using the forefinger and thumb as manipulators and the remaining fingers as aids. The weapon can briefly be held firmly when parrying or thrusting, but otherwise the hand should be relaxed or the muscles will tire quickly.

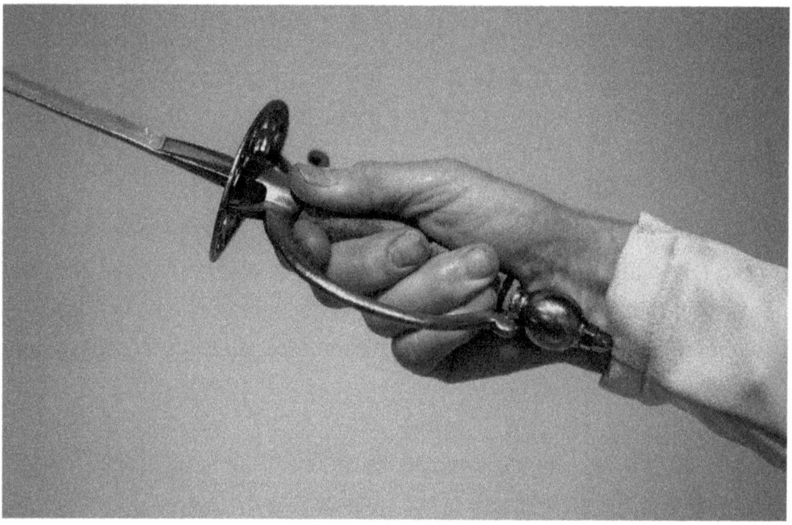

The recommended hold.

2.3 The Stance

This is similar to the modern foil stance. Place your feet two foot lengths apart and at right angles, with the front foot in line with the back heel. Turn your torso at an angle to your opponent. Bend your knees so they are vertically above your toes. The French style of smallsword fencing included putting most of the weight on the back leg and leaning somewhat backwards. Possibly this was influenced by the need to protect the head in the days before masks were worn. Apparently, the Italians kept the weight evenly balanced over both legs. There is likely no advantage in adopting the French stance, which has now gone out of fashion and risks over-stressing the back knee. In my opinion, the modern stance with the weight balanced equally over both legs is superior. The illustrations in the old manuals do not show the knees bent as much as is normal in modern fencing.

The sword arm should be straighter than at foil and more elevated, the wrist at chest height or a little lower than the shoulder, the blade angled

The stance: the fencer on the left is on guard in tierce; the fencer on the right is in sixte.

up at about 15 degrees. This should be balanced by the other arm held up and behind, with the upper arm horizontal and the lower arm upright to be comfortably balanced or behind the vertical to adhere more strictly to the illustrations in the old manuals, and the wrist should be relaxed. Modern fencers have become lazy about the way they hold this arm, but when held correctly, it does aid balance if it is thrown back when lunging and brought back up when recovering from a lunge.

2.4 Gaining and Breaking Ground

The normal way of advancing is to take a short step forwards of about six inches with the front foot, followed by a similar step with the back foot. To gain more ground, bring the back heel up to the front heel, and then take a similarly sized step forwards with the front foot.

To retire, the normal practice is to step back about six inches with the back foot, followed by a similar step back with the front foot. One can also bring the front heel back to the back heel, and then take a similar step back with the back foot. Another possibility is to spring backwards from both feet simultaneously.

Note that while most movements in a bout will be forwards and backwards, sideways steps are also permitted.

2.5 The Fencing Measure

This is the distance between a fencer and his opponent. It is correct when the opponent can be hit when attacking with a lunge so that the blade bends as if it could have penetrated about three inches. The measure will need to be adjusted continually as the opponent moves in or out of distance. The correct measure will likely be different for both fencers if they are of different heights. To adjust the measure, it is not necessary to take the same number of steps as the opponent; the measure can be corrected with as many or as few steps as required.

2.6 The Principle of Defence

The principle of defence is the opposition of forte to foible. Even a weak fencer can easily deflect a strong fencer's foible with the forte, whereas there is not enough strength in the weaker foible to dominate an opponent's blade.

2.7 Guard Positions

Being *on guard* means you are ready to defend yourself. Some of the old manuals recommend a centralised guard position so that the defender has only a short distance sideways to move the sword to effect a simple parry on whichever side of the blade an attack is launched. This is probably a hangover from the days of heavier swords when a simple parry was the only practical option. With lighter, faster swords, however, other parries are possible, and the recommendation now is to adopt a position such that one part of the body is completely protected. Depending on which side of the blade an attack is launched, it is referred to as an attack to the inside or the outside.

If fencers come on guard with swords crossed, then only one fencer can be completely covered, but only a small movement is necessary to parry a direct thrust should one be attempted. If one fencer moves the sword across to close the line completely, it presents an opportunity for the opponent to launch an indirect attack (see section 2.11).

Prime.

Prime. This defends the upper inside part of the body. The hand is held in pronation at shoulder height with the blade angled a little forwards of the vertical. This may seem awkward at first for the modern fencer, but it is particularly useful against an opponent who forces a way in against a blade held in tierce, and it is well worth practising. Prime can also parry an attack in the quarte line – from tierce, drop the blade down and then move the hand across. Do not turn the blade in a semicircle or it will snag on the opponent's blade. One disadvantage of the prime position is that quick ripostes are not easy to execute. Angelo notes that the prime position was known as St. George. This refers to Joseph Bologne, Chevalier de Saint-Georges, who was a virtuoso violinist, composer and conductor, and was also regarded as the finest swordsman of his day.

Seconde. This protects the outside of the body below the wrist. The hand is held at shoulder height in pronation, the point angled down towards the opponent's waist. The seconde parry can defend against thrusts in seconde, septime and octave.

Seconde.

Tierce. This defends the outside of the body above the wrist, the hand in pronation at chest height, the blade angled up at about 15 degrees, The tierce parry can defend against thrusts in tierce or sixte.

Tierce.

Quarte. This defends the inside of the body above the wrist. The hand is held in semi-supination at chest height, the blade angled up at about 15 degrees. The quarte parry can defend against thrusts in quarte. The hand can also be lowered to parry thrusts in septime, octave and seconde.

Quarte.

Sixte. This is the same as tierce but with the hand in semi-supination.

Septime. This defends the inside of the body below the wrist, the hand in supination at shoulder height,

Sixte.

Septime.

the blade angled down towards the opponent's waist. Although more usually used to parry thrusts below the wrist, septime can also defend against thrusts in tierce, quarte and sixte.

Octave. This is the same as seconde but with the hand in supination.

Octave.

To remember which position is prime and which is seconde, it can help to visualise prime as being the first position a sword might be in after drawing it from the scabbard. Septime and octave are sometimes confused: in septime, the lower arm and the sword form a pattern a bit like a figure 7.

In the smallsword era, swordsmen often had to defend themselves against cutting weapons. Prime, seconde and tierce, with the hand in pronation, provide a stronger defence against cuts. Tierce is used in preference to sixte in the old manuals. While they are not taught in modern foil fencing, parries with the hand in pronation provide a stronger defence against a forceful opponent.

Note that quinte is missing from the above list. This guard position is now defined (for the foil and épée) as a low quarte with the hand held lower than normal and the point higher than the wrist. This position is not mentioned in the old fencing manuals, but in practice, it is sometimes used in panic when septime would have been more appropriate. Neuvieme, a modern parry introduced as a defence against flick hits, is not relevant in the context of smallsword fencing, so this has not been listed either.

2.8 Attacks Above and Below the Wrist

With the smallsword, the distinction is not between high and low lines as with modern foil, but above and below the wrist. Thrusts below the wrist (prime, seconde, septime, octave) will also arrive in a high position because the smallsword user's wrist will be higher than the modern foilist's. A thrust in septime, for example, is like a thrust in quarte but delivered below the wrist.

2.9 Lines of Attack

A thrust in ...

- **Prime** is to the inside below the wrist with the hand in pronation.
- **Seconde** is to the outside below the wrist with the hand in pronation.
- **Tierce** is to the outside above the wrist with the hand in pronation.
- **Quarte** is to the inside above the wrist with the hand in semi-supination.
- **Sixte** is to the outside above the wrist with the hand in semi-supination.

- **Septime** is to the inside below the wrist with the hand in supination.
- **Octave** is to the outside below the wrist with the hand in supination.

Since the blades are more usually engaged in the higher guard positions, when attacking below the wrist there is usually no opposing blade present, so what is the difference between attacks in septime and octave? It's only really a technicality that distinguishes them: it depends which side the attacker raises the hand to cover. Covering is to the attacker's outside for attacks in seconde and octave, and to the inside for attacks in septime. When there is a call for a thrust below the wrist in the exercises or fight sequences in the following chapters, just remember to hold the hand in pronation for prime and seconde and in supination for septime and octave, cover into the opposing blade, and you will be delivering the required thrust.

2.10 Types of Parry

It is worth remembering that the arm is always bent when taking a parry but straightened when making a thrust.

- **The simple parry.** The sword is carried laterally over to the opposite side of the body, keeping the blade parallel to its starting position. For example, from tierce to quarte, or from octave to septime. This is an instinctive parry that comes naturally, though by instinct, it is usually executed badly. When fencers are allowed to fight before they have been taught the acquired parries, this is the only one they will attempt. It is sometimes performed in a wild uncontrolled manner, resulting in the fencer smashing across and down, and finally hitting the floor with the point if the opponent's blade is not found. This parry must be executed in a calm, controlled manner, and should move just enough to deflect the attacking blade some four inches past the target.
- **The counter or circular parry.** As the name suggests, the point of the blade traces a complete circle to gather up the opponent's blade. In

sixte/tierce and septime, the motion is clockwise, while in quarte and octave/seconde, it is anticlockwise. The blade should end up back in the exact same position where it started. The arm should not move when executing this parry. Where possible it should be done entirely with the fingers without moving the wrist. This is easy to do when the hand is in supination or semi-supination. In pronation, more assistance from the wrist may be required. The advantage of using the fingers is that bringing the sword back to its starting position is much easier, as the sword grip merely has to return to its original position in the hand. The circle should be as small as possible so it can be effected quickly. This parry is easiest when the opponent's blade is close to the parrying blade – the greater the separation, the wider the circle needed to gather the blade.

- **The semicircular parry.** Here the blade is curved inwards from a higher to a lower guard (or vice versa) on the same side, for example, from quarte to septime, or from octave to sixte. This parry is executed by turning the wrist. The lower arm is allowed to twist, but its position must not change throughout the semicircle. One common fault is to circle the wrong way and then move the hand across to the other side of the body on discovering that the parry has been unsuccessful.
- **The ceding or yielding parry.** Here, the idea is to give way to an attacking blade that is in contact with yours and, using an arm movement and to pivot your blade around the blade contact point, bringing your forte against your opponent's foible and deflecting it away from the target. Faced with a forced attack in tierce, lowering the blade and moving the hand across into prime is an easy option. A forced attack from sixte to septime (see the bind, section 2.15) can be parried by circling the hand inwards, over and round the attacking blade, taking it back into tierce. Similarly, a forced attack from quarte into octave (bind) can be parried by circling round the blade back into quarte. When taking a ceding parry, the blade must not lose contact with the opponent's blade. One can feel by the contact on the blade when a ceding parry is possible, and it can be taken almost subconsciously when conditions feel just right.

2.11 Types of Attack or Riposte

- **The direct or straight thrust.** This is difficult to bring off as an attack, as it is very easily parried. A fast direct riposte, however, is often successful.
- **The indirect thrust.** This is a thrust preceded by a simple disengage or a cut-over to an open line. The attacker should close the line into the opponent's blade as the hit is made to guard against a direct riposte.

A disengage is performed by dropping the point under the opposing blade and bringing it up on the other side. The movement should be small and neat. It can be effected with finger play – for example, when the hand is in semi-supination, relax the grip on the last three fingers (the aids), push with the thumb and pull with the forefinger (the manipulators) to move the blade down, and then push with the finger and pull with the thumb to lift the blade up on the opposite side. Finally, close the aids to locate the grip securely in the hand.

A cut-over is performed by raising the forearm, causing the blade to slide up along the opponent's blade until the point is cleared, and then lowering the forearm again with the blade on the opposite side.

- **The counter-disengagement.** This attack is initiated when the defender disengages and changes from one line to another. In time with the defender, the attacker disengages back to the original line and launches an attack as the defender moves across to the opposite line.
- **The compound attack or riposte.** This is a thrust in which the final line of attack is preceded by one or more feint attacks, designed to draw a parry from the opponent that can be deceived.

A feint attack is made by straightening the sword arm forcibly in a convincing manner to provoke the parry. The attacker must synchronise with the opponent's timing to deceive the parry without making any blade contact. When practising, the defender executes the parry as soon as the attacker's arm is straightened, and the attacker lunges after changing engagement to the final line. When fighting, the defender should delay the parry to the last moment to make it harder for the attacker to succeed with a compound attack. This means that the attacker needs to make the attack 'progressive' by performing the final deception while on the lunge – this is not easy to do at first and requires some practice. The lunge must be controlled so that forward progression is relatively slow initially, and the final part can speed up as the final deception is completed. To control the speed, the weight needs to be on the rear leg, which needs to have a good bend at the knee.

A feint of a disengage followed by another disengage to deceive a simple parry is known as a *one-two*, and a feint of a disengage followed by a counter-disengage to deceive a counter-parry is known as a *doublé*.

- **The cavé.** This is a risky attack in the open line that is no longer taught. Instead of attacking with opposition, this is the direct opposite – the hand is moved well away from the opponent's blade. Attacking to the inside, which is more usual, the hand is held in pronation, whereas it is held in supination for attacks to the outside. It might be used, for example, in an attempt to get around a parry, but without closing into the blade, there is a risk of provoking a time-hit or causing a double hit from a fast riposte. Sidestepping before making the thrust would make it less risky.

2.12 Making a Thrust

- All thrusts are made by first extending the arm and then lunging if necessary. The hand must be raised high enough to enable covering into the opponent's blade. If the latter is in the recommended position, the hand will need to be at head height when attacking.

Attack in quarte, the hand raised above shoulder level and covering into the opposing blade.

- When a successful attack is made with a lunge, the hit should arrive as the front foot lands on the ground.
- The back foot should remain flat on the ground when lunging. The attacker pushes off from the rear edge of the foot. The toe of the leading foot is raised before the heel, and the foot just clears the ground as the rear leg drives the body forwards. The leading foot remains below the knee during the lunge and lands heel first. The upper body retains its upright position throughout. To recover from the lunge, the toe of the leading foot is raised and the fencer returns to guard by pushing off from the heel while bending the rear knee. A lunge is incorrect if the fencer lifts the leading foot and then merely falls forwards under gravity, on the contrary, it must be controlled by taking the weight in the rear leg and driving the body forwards.
- All hits are made with the hand higher than the point, whether attacking above or below the wrist.

- The left arm should be thrown back for balance when lunging and, ideally, the left hand should match the right, for example, when attacking in sixte or quarte, the palm should be uppermost. However, when attacking in tierce or seconde, the palm should be turned face down. The arm is raised back up as the attacker recovers from the lunge.

2.13 Counter-attacks

It is called a counter-attack when the defender launches an attack instead of parrying an incoming thrust. Often this leads to bad fencing, but it can work if the defender can be certain he won't receive a hit.

- **The time-hit.** This is a counter-attack where the final line of the attack is anticipated and intercepted. A period of fencing time is gained by replacing the parry and riposte with a single action.
- **The stop-hit.** A counter-attack that, as the name suggests, prevents the attack from arriving. The big risk with this is that the counter-attack may arrive first but not succeed in stopping the attack from arriving, which, in smallsword fencing, counts as a double hit.

Counter-attacks made in lieu of parrying with no intention of intercepting the attack or stopping it arriving are simply bad swordsmanship and have no place in smallsword fencing. These are a favourite ploy of the épéeist who plans for his counter-attack to arrive ahead of the attack so he can score a point. The fact that he is hit a fraction of a second later is of no concern to him.

- **Counter-time** can be used against an opponent who stop hits instead of parrying. This is the action of drawing the stop-hit, parrying it and riposting.

2.14 Renewed Attacks

- **The remise.** This is executed on the lunge by replacing the point on the target after it has been parried. Not to be attempted if a direct riposte from the opponent is likely or it will probably result in a double hit. Typically, it can be used against a defender who initiates a disengage riposte, particularly from quarte into the tierce line, without waiting for the attacker to bend the arm and start recovering to guard. Even then, there is a risk of a double hit.
- **The redoublement.** This attack is made on the lunge with one or more blade movements after the initial attack has failed. This could be used when an opponent parries and then pauses instead of riposting, but it must never be used in place of parrying a riposte.
- **The reprise.** This is a second lunge performed after recovering from an initial lunge and returning to guard. There are two varieties: a reprise to the rear and a reprise forwards. In the reprise to the rear, the recovery is done in the normal way by bringing the front leg back, before lunging again. The second lunge can be started before the leading foot has quite landed on the ground in the on guard position. In a reprise forwards, the recovery is performed by bringing the back leg forwards to the guard position before lunging again. It can be used to gain ground on a retreating opponent.

2.15 Takings of the Blade

Often referred to by the French term *prises de fer*, these blade manipulations are always performed against a straight arm, keeping the forte in contact with the opponent's foible.

- **The envelopment.** This is normally done in sixte and performed by making a complete circle revolving around the opponent's blade, plus a few degrees more, without losing contact. It cannot be easily attempted in quarte, as the opponent's blade is likely to snag on the sword arm.

- **The bind.** This is the action of taking the opponent's blade diagonally from an upper guard on one side to a lower guard on the opposite side, or vice versa. It might perhaps be done after a parry, for example, to take the blade from sixte to septime, or from octave to quarte. The bind can be executed smoothly or rapidly moving forwards with a flick, which can sometimes disarm the opponent.
- **The croisé.** Crossing the blades. Taking the blade from high line to low line on the same side, the point to be kept higher than the guard. This is usually done following a quarte parry when the recovery is delayed. Jean Olivier, in *Fencing Familiarized*, 1771, has it executed quickly and forcefully, the hand turned to pronation, with the aim of disarming the opponent. More recently, Roger Crosnier in *Fencing with the Foil* describes it as being executed more gently, with the hand turned to supination to trap the opponent's blade while riposting.
- **The flanconade.** This obsolete thrust was like a croisé but executed with the point lower than the guard. Performed against a straight arm in quarte, the blade was taken over from the inside to the outside of the opponent's blade and kept in the quarte line. As the opponent's blade was not well trapped by the guard, the left hand was typically used to deflect it outwards as the thrust was made to the flank. This movement was already becoming obsolete in the eighteenth century - Olivier preferred a bind into octave and advised against using the left hand.

2.16 Preparations for an Attack

- **The coulé.** In the old fencing manuals this is given the English translation *glizard*. It is the action of sliding, or grazing the attacker's blade along the opponent's blade.
- **The pressure.** Here the attacker presses laterally against the opponent's blade, either to dislodge it to make an opening or to provoke a reaction from which an advantage can be taken.

- **The beat.** This is a smart tap against the opponent's blade to dislodge it or provoke a reaction from which an advantage can be taken. Care must be taken to control the beat so as not to overshoot if the opponent manages to evade the contact.
- **The froissement.** This is rather like a combined pressure and coulé. It is performed by pushing strongly against the opponent's blade while sliding forwards against it. This is not covered in the exercises.

2.17 The Flying Cut-over

This can be used following a parry of prime. It is a large movement consisting of three-quarters of a vertical circle, formed by taking the blade rapidly down and back, then up and forwards into quarte. It needs the element of surprise, as there is a moment after clearing the opponent's blade when you are unprotected from the point of the sword.

2.18 The Pass

This is an alternative to the lunge as a means of reaching the opponent. The sword arm is straightened first, then the left foot steps about two feet ahead of the right foot, pointing out slightly, and the fencer straightens the right knee, taking weight off the heel of the right foot. The left knee can be straightened (Angelo) or bent (Girard). Recovering to guard from the pass is not so easy as from the lunge. The pass has been discarded in modern fencing, but it has some use in smallsword fencing, as it brings the left hand closer to the opponent's blade, which can be useful, and it can take the opponent by surprise.

2.19 The Demi-volte

This is an evasive action taken against an attack by turning the body anticlockwise away from the line of the attack, pivoting the left foot over behind the right foot and straightening the legs. It also provides an opportunity for straightening the sword arm and delivering a thrust.

2.20 Rules of Engagement

There are no universally agreed rules of combat for smallsword fencing, but, typically, fencers are not restricted to a piste – the whole body is a target, and use of the left hand is permitted for parrying, deflecting or grabbing the opponent's blade, so a glove is needed on the left hand. Grabbing the blade was not recommended but it did happen in duels. Use of the left hand effectively puts a stop to those nasty close-quarter jabs that are so often seen on the competition piste.

The treatment of double hits, which differs from that used in sports fencing, fosters good swordsmanship by taking account of who would get hurt in a duel: if both fencers are hit in the same period of fencing time, it counts as a double hit, even if one hit arrives before the other. It is not possible to recreate duelling conditions exactly in a recreational context, but in practice, this means that if the second person to hit starts making a thrust before receiving a hit, it counts as a double hit. However, if this thrust doesn't begin until after a hit has been received, it is ignored for scoring purposes, with the assumption that in a duel the fencer would not have been able to continue. When scoring, a double hit should penalise both fencers, perhaps by clearing both scores to zero or knocking both fencers out of the contest.

Some fencers may find it hard to adapt to the smallsword, as they are inclined to launch counter-attacks instead of parrying in the hope of scoring a hit first. This is suicidal with the smallsword unless a stop-hit actually succeeds in preventing the attack from arriving. It is much safer to parry an attack.

Since there is some potential for getting hurt once blades have been grabbed, my recommendation is that a hit made immediately after the blade is held should be allowed, but thereafter there should be no more grappling; the fight should be stopped and the fencers put back on guard.

The implication of the old manuals is that the fencer's blades were usually engaged, which I recommend. This was normal practice, not only in the smallsword era but also right up until quite recently. Contact with the opponent's blade adds feeling (*sentiment du fer*, as the French call it) to the visual perception and enables some actions that have been largely lost due to the modern predilection for fighting with 'absence of blade'.

Chapter 3

Exercises for the Smallsword

I have derived many of the exercises described here from John MacArthur's 1780 publication *Theory and Practice of Fencing*. MacArthur was a student of Jean Olivier, so it is likely that these exercises were practised in his school. I have also included some input from Domenico Angelo (1763), P. J. F. Girard (1740), my fencing instructor Alan Wolsoncroft and myself. The early fencing publications were written for the foil when it was a practice weapon for the smallsword. Many of the exercises can be easily adapted for the modern foil for those who are interested in learning the old traditional fencing skills.

Coaches may wish to break the exercises down further for pupils. For example, to ensure that they straighten the sword arm first when attacking, it could be: '1, disengage, 2, straighten the arm, 3, lunge'.

Note that further variations can be constructed from these basic notes, for example by including advancing and retiring, or keeping the attacker on the lunge while the parry and riposte are performed. It is not a bad idea to repeat the exercises with the sword in the other hand. This will obviously feel more awkward, but if ever you are unable to use your sword arm for any reason, it does mean you don't have to stop fencing. Some of the old masters recommended learning to fence with both hands.

- The two fencers are labelled A and B.
- Begin the exercises slowly, and gradually build up to fighting speed.
- Swap round so that fencer A is now fencer B and fencer B is fencer A. Repeat.

- Novice fencers will need supervision to ensure that they perform the exercises correctly, and it's best if they can partner a more experienced fencer so that at least one of them should get it right.
- The exercises are designed as practice for the thrusts, parries, etc., which should be used when fighting.

3.1 Target Practice

- Set up a pad on a wall with a spot to aim at, and practise attacking with a lunge and hitting it. Try attacks starting from each of the various guard positions. Remember to straighten the arm before lunging, which makes aiming a lot easier. This exercise not only improves accuracy but also aids learning the correct fencing measure.
- Since the arm is a valid target with the smallsword, it is a useful exercise if one fencer exposes various parts of his forearm by raising it, lowering it, or moving it to one side or the other so the opponent can then try to hit it when attacking with a lunge.

Note that the exercise called *thrusting at the wall*, which is mentioned in some of the old fencing manuals, is not literally about thrusting at a wall. Instead, the idea is to attack another fencer, who must stand still on the spot without moving, as if his back were against a wall. This gives the defender an opportunity to practise parrying.

3.2 Mastering the Guard Positions

Stand in front of a mirror and check your position as you adopt each of the guard positions. Switch back and forth between any two positions, checking each time that the position is correct. Try one or more circular movements in all but prime, as if you were taking counter-parries, Ensure that your position after each circle is unchanged from the starting position.

3.3 Successive Changes of Engagement Between Tierce and Quarte, Terminated by a Counter-disengage Attack

Begin with blades engaged in tierce.

1. The opponent of the fencer changing engagement should stay covered by changing line to quarte or tierce at the same time and should finish the sequence with a counter-disengage attack.
2. Same exercise with the fencer changing lines stepping forwards on every change, and the opponent stepping back.
3. Same exercise with the fencer changing lines stepping back on every change, and the opponent stepping forwards.

3.4 Direct and Indirect Ripostes

1. Engage blades in quarte
   - **A** Exert pressure on B's blade
   - **B** Disengage attack in tierce, stay on the lunge
   - **A** Parry tierce, extend the arm and riposte in tierce or seconde
2. Engage blades in tierce
   - **A** Exert pressure on B's blade
   - **B** Disengage attack in quarte, stay on the lunge
   - **A** Parry quarte, extend the arm and riposte in quarte
3. Engage blades in quarte
   - **A** Exert pressure on B's blade
   - **B** Disengage attack in tierce
   - **A** Parry tierce
   - **B** Recover to tierce
   - **A** Disengage riposte in quarte

4. Engage blades in tierce
   - A exert pressure on B's blade
   - B Disengage attack in quarte
   - A Parry quarte
   - B Recover to quarte
   - A Disengage riposte in tierce

3.5 Preparation With Pressure

Engage blades in quarte, the attacker A to exert a strong pressure on the defender's blade, then:

1. B gives way to the pressure, and A delivers a straight thrust and hits in quarte
2. B resists the pressure, and A delivers a disengage attack and hits in tierce
3. First counter-riposte by disengagement
   - B Resist the pressure from A's blade
   - A Disengage attack in sixte
   - B Simple parry of tierce, direct riposte
   - A Parry sixte and disengage riposte and hit in quarte as B returns to guard in sixte
4. Attack with a one-two
   - B resist the pressure from A's blade
   - A feint of disengage to tierce, disengage to quarte
   - B simple parry of tierce, which is deceived

3.6 A Sequence of Successive Simple Parries and Indirect Ripostes, Terminated With a One–Two Riposte

Begin with blades engaged in quarte and a disengage attack from A in tierce. B parries tierce and delivers a disengage riposte in quarte as A recovers to tierce. A parries quarte and delivers a disengage riposte in tierce as B recovers to quarte. The sequence repeats until B decides to deliver a one-two riposte and hit.

3.7 Sequences of Simple Quarte, Counter-quarte and Septime Parries

Engage blades in tierce, then A disengages and attacks in quarte.

1. Successive simple quarte parries and direct ripostes until B hits with a disengage riposte.
2. As with 1, but continue with A parrying the riposte with counter-quarte and disengage riposte. Successive counter-parries and disengage ripostes until B hits with a doublé riposte.
3. As with 1, but continue with A parrying the riposte with septime and riposting in septime. Successive septime parries and septime ripostes until B disengages over the blade to hit in octave.

3.8 Septime

1. Engage blades in quarte, disengage attack in septime
2. Engage blades in tierce
   - **A** Disengage attack in quarte
   - **B** Parry quarte, riposte in septime
3. Engage blades in quarte
   - **A** Disengage attack in tierce
   - **B** Parry tierce, disengage riposte in quarte
   - **A** Parry quarte, riposte septime
4. As 3, but continue thus:
   - **B** Parry septime, riposte in septime
   - **A** Parry septime, riposte and hit in septime

5. Engage blades in quarte
   - A Disengage attack in sixte
   - B Parry septime, riposte septime
   - A Parry septime, riposte quarte
   - B Parry quarte, riposte and hit in septime
6. Engage blades in quarte
   - A Change line to tierce
   - B Feint disengage to quarte
   - A Parry quarte, which is deceived
   - B Attack and hit in septime
7. Engage blades in tierce
   - A Put pressure on B's blade
   - B Disengage, attack and hit in septime
8. As 7 above, but continue thus: a parry septime, riposte and hit in quarte
9. Engage blades in quarte
   - A Advance, disengage attack in tierce
   - B Retreat, parry tierce
   - A Recover to tierce pressing against the blade
   - B Disengage riposte and hit in septime
10. Engage blades in quarte
    - A Feint sixte, disengage attack and hit in septime
    - B Parry tierce, which is deceived
11. Engage blades in quarte
    - A Retreat
    - B Advance, disengage attack in sixte
    - A Simple parry sixte
    - B Recover to sixte
    - A Disengage riposte to quarte
    - B Simple parry quarte, direct riposte to quarte
    - A Simple parry quarte, stay there without riposting
    - B Renewed attack and hit septime

12. Engage blades in quarte
    - **A** Disengage attack in septime
    - **B** Parry septime, bind to tierce, direct riposte and hit

3.9 Octave

1. Engage blades in sixte, attack and hit in octave
2. Engage blades in sixte
    - **A** Attack in octave
    - **B** Parry octave, riposte in octave
3. Engage blades in quarte
    - **A** Disengage attack to tierce
    - **B** Simple parry tierce, reverse the wrist to riposte octave
4. Engage blades in quarte
    - **A** Attack in septime
    - **B** Parry septime
    - **A** Recover to septime
    - **B** Disengage and riposte in octave
5. As 4 above, but continue thus:
    - **A** Parry octave
    - **B** Recover to octave
    - **A** Disengage, riposte and hit in septime
6. Engage blades in tierce
    - **A** Straight thrust in tierce
    - **B** Parry tierce, feint direct riposte
    - **A** Recover to tierce
    - **B** Disengage, riposte and hit in octave
7. Engage blades in tierce
    - **A** Disengage attack in quarte and stay there
    - **B** Parry quarte, bind to octave, riposte and hit in octave

8. Engage blades in tierce
   - A Disengage attack in quarte
   - B Simple parry quarte, bind to octave, feint direct riposte to octave
   - A Recover to octave
   - B Disengage, riposte and hit in sixte
9. Engage blades in tierce
   - A Disengage attack in quarte
   - B Simple parry quarte, bind to octave, riposte to octave
   - A Ceding parry to quarte, riposte and hit in septime

3.10 Prime and Seconde

1. Engage blades in tierce
   - A Advance and thrust strongly in tierce
   - B Parry prime, riposte in prime
2. Engage blades in tierce
   - A Advance and thrust strongly in tierce
   - B Parry prime and use the left hand to deflect A's blade, riposte in prime

Using the left hand to deflect the blade while riposting after parrying prime.

3. Engage blades in tierce
   - **A** Advance and thrust strongly in tierce
   - **B** While parrying prime, sidestep, taking first the right foot and then the left foot sideways, and riposte in seconde
4. Engage blades in tierce
   - **A** Advance and thrust strongly in tierce
   - **B** Parry prime, bind to sixte, riposte and hit in sixte
5. Engage blades in tierce
   - **A** Advance and thrust strongly in tierce
   - **B** Parry prime, flying cut over to quarte and hit
6. Engage blades in tierce
   - **A** Advance and thrust strongly in tierce
   - **B** Parry prime, riposte in prime
   - **A** Parry prime, riposte and hit in prime
7. Engage blades in tierce
   - **A** Advance and disengage attack in quarte
   - **B** Parry prime
   - **A** Recover to septime
   - **B** Disengage, riposte and hit in seconde
8. Engage blades in quarte
   - **A** Disengage attack in sixte
   - **B** Parry tierce, direct riposte of tierce
   - **A** Parry tierce
   - **B** Recover to tierce
   - **A** Advance and thrust strongly in tierce
   - **B** Parry prime, riposte and hit in prime
9. Engage blades in quarte
   - **A** Disengage attack in sixte
   - **B** Parry tierce, direct riposte in tierce
   - **A** Parry tierce, riposte strongly in tierce
   - **B** Parry prime
   - **A** Recover to septime
   - **B** Disengage riposte and hit in seconde

3.11 Seconde

1. Engage blades in tierce
   - A Disengage attack in seconde
   - B Parry seconde, direct riposte and hit in seconde

Attack in seconde and parry of seconde.

2. Engage blades in quarte
   - A Disengage attack in sixte
   - B Parry tierce, riposte and hit in seconde
3. Engage blades in tierce
   - A Feint to seconde, disengage attack and hit in sixte
   - B Parry seconde, which is deceived
4. Engage blades in quarte
   - A Exert pressure against B's blade
   - B Close the line in quarte
   - A Disengage attack in sixte
   - B Parry tierce
   - A Recover to tierce, continuing to press against B's blade
   - B Disengage, riposte and hit in seconde

Ceding parry of tierce against a thrust in septime.

5. Engage blades in tierce
   - A Attack in seconde
   - B Parry seconde, riposte in seconde
   - A Parry seconde
   - B Recover to seconde
   - A Disengage, riposte and hit in seconde
6. Engage blades in quarte
   - A Disengage attack in tierce
   - B Simple parry tierce, bind to septime and riposte
   - A Ceding parry to tierce, riposte and hit in seconde
7. Engage blades in tierce
   - A Disengage attack in quarte and stay there
   - B Parry quarte, bind to seconde keeping the hand at shoulder height, riposte and hit in seconde

3.12 Compound Attacks

The initial feint must be made with a straight arm. These exercises can be done in two ways. Firstly, the defender is to react to the straightened arm by parrying, and the attacker then deceives this parry. Secondly, and much harder, the defender should delay the parry until the attacker is already on the lunge, and the attacker must deceive the parry while on the lunge.

1. One-two attack from tierce or quarte, deceiving a parry of quarte or tierce.
2. Feint high, disengage below the wrist, from quarte or tierce, deceiving a tierce or quarte parry.
3. Feint below the wrist, disengage above the wrist, from tierce or quarte, deceiving a parry of seconde or septime.
4. Doublé attack from tierce or quarte, deceiving a counter parry.
5. One-two-three attack from tierce or quarte, deceiving two simple parries.
6. Doublé counter-disengage attack from tierce or quarte deceiving two counter-parries.

3.13 Counter-parries of Tierce and Quarte

1. Counter-quarte direct riposte, starting with blades engaged in quarte
   - A Disengage attack in sixte
   - B Parry counter-quarte, direct riposte and hit
2. Counter-quarte, indirect riposte, starting with blades engaged in quarte
   - A Disengage attack in sixte
   - B Parry counter-quarte
   - A Recover to quarte
   - B Indirect riposte and hit in sixte
3. As 2, but continue thus:
   - A Parry counter-quarte, direct riposte in quarte
   - B Simple parry of quarte
   - A Recover to quarte
   - B Indirect riposte and hit in sixte
4. Counter-tierce, direct riposte, starting with blades engaged in tierce
   - A Disengage attack in quarte
   - B Parry counter-tierce, direct riposte and hit
5. Counter-tierce, indirect riposte, starting with blades engaged in tierce
   - A Disengage attack in quarte
   - B Parry counter-tierce
   - A Recover to tierce
   - B Indirect riposte and hit in quarte
6. As 5, but continue thus:
   - A Parry counter-tierce, direct riposte in tierce
   - B Simple parry of tierce
   - A Recover to tierce
   - B Indirect riposte and hit in quarte
7. Doublé riposte, starting with blades engaged in quarte
   - A Disengage attack in sixte
   - B Parry counter-quarte, doublé riposte and hit
   - A Recover to quarte and parry counter-quarte, which is deceived

8. Feint high, disengage low starting with blades engaged in tierce
   - **A** Disengage attack in quarte
   - **B** Parry counter-tierce
   - **A** Counter-disengage below the wrist and hit in seconde
9. Feint high, disengage low starting with blades engaged in quarte
   - **A** Disengage attack in tierce
   - **B** Parry counter-quarte
   - **A** Counter-disengage and hit in octave
10. Deceiving a counter-parry and a simple parry, starting with blades engaged in quarte
   - **A** Attack by doublé, and disengage to quarte and hit
   - **B** Parry counter-quarte then tierce, both of which are deceived

3.14 Counter-parries of Septime and Octave

1. Engage blades in quarte
   - **A** Disengage attack in septime
   - **B** Parry septime,
   - **A** Recover to septime
   - **B** Disengage riposte to octave
   - **A** Counter-parry of septime
   - **B** Recover to septime
   - **A** Disengage riposte to octave and hit
2. Engage blades in sixte
   - **A** Disengage attack in octave
   - **B** Parry octave
   - **A** Recover to octave
   - **B** Disengage riposte to septime
   - **A** Counter-parry of octave
   - **B** Recover to octave
   - **A** Disengage riposte to septime and hit

3.15 The Time-hit

Time-hits are difficult to execute and are best attempted against a fencer who attacks with the hand too low and doesn't cover into the opposing blade, thereby leaving some target exposed - which is what fencer A should do for these exercises.

1. Engage blades in quarte
   - **A** Disengage attack in sixte
   - **B** Simultaneously with the disengage, parry sixte, extend the arm and hit
2. Engage blades in quarte
   - **A** One-two attack, feint disengage in sixte, disengage attack in quarte
   - **B** The first parry of sixte only partially complete, enough to provoke the second disengagement to quarte, then as the disengagement is made, cover into the blade, extend the arm, attack and hit in quarte

The time-hit: The fencer on the right has attacked without raising his hand above his shoulder, which has exposed his target to the time-hit from the left.

3. Same exercise starting with blades engaged in tierce
   - **A** One–two attack, feint disengage in quarte, disengage attack in tierce
   - **B** The first parry of quarte only partially complete, enough to provoke the second disengagement to tierce, then as the disengagement is made, cover into the blade, extend the arm, attack and hit in sixte
4. Engage blades in quarte
   - **A** Disengage beat attack
   - **B** Counter-quarte and time-hit in quarte
5. Engage blades in quarte
   - **A** Press strongly on the blade and straighten the arm
   - **B** Disengage and time-hit in sixte
6. Engage blades in quarte
   - **A** Retreat
   - **B** Advance with a disengage, press strongly on the blade in sixte and straighten the arm
   - **A** Disengage and time-hit in quarte
7. Engage blades in sixte
   - **A** Attack in octave
   - **B** Time-hit in octave

3.16 The Cut-over

Note: the cut-over is easier to execute when the opponent holds the guard low and the point high.

1. Engage blades in quarte. A cut-over, attack and hit in sixte
2. Engage blades in tierce. A Cut-over, attack and hit in quarte
3. Engage blades in quarte
   - **A** one–two attack by cut-over, disengage
   - **B** Simple parry of tierce, which is deceived

4. Change engagement by cut-over then attack by cut-over, starting with blades engaged in quarte
   - A Change line to tierce by cut-over
   - B Change line to tierce
   - A Cut-over, attack and hit in quarte
5. Change engagement by cut-over, then attack by cut-over, starting with blades engaged in sixte
   - A Change line to quarte by cut-over
   - B Change line to quarte
   - A Cut-over, attack and hit in sixte
6. Change engagement twice by cut-over, then disengage attack, starting with blades engaged in tierce
   - A Change line to quarte by cut-over
   - B Change line to quarte
   - A Change line to tierce by cut-over
   - B Change line to tierce
   - A Disengage, attack and hit in quarte
7. Cut-over to change engagement, followed by a one–two attack, starting with blades engaged in quarte
   - A Change line to tierce by cut-over
   - B Change line to tierce
   - A One–two attack and hit in sixte
   - B Simple parry of quarte on the first feint, which is deceived
8. Cut-over to change engagement, followed by a one–two attack, starting with blades engaged in tierce
   - A Change line to quarte by cut-over
   - B Change line to quarte
   - A One–two attack and hit in quarte
   - B Simple parry of tierce on the first feint, which is deceived
9. Doublé attack from quarte, the feint by cut-over
   - A Cut-over and feint sixte
   - B Parry counter-quarte, which is deceived
   - A Counter-disengage and hit in sixte

10. Doublé attack from tierce, the feint by cut-over
    - A Cut-over and feint quarte
    - B Parry counter-tierce, which is deceived
    - A Counter-disengage and hit in quarte
11. Feint high by cut-over, disengage low, starting with blades engaged in quarte
    - A Cut-over and feint sixte
    - B Simple parry of tierce, which is deceived
    - A Disengage and hit in octave
12. Feint high by cut-over, disengage low, starting with blades engaged in tierce
    - A Cut-over and feint quarte,
    - B Simple parry of quarte, which is deceived
    - A Disengage and hit in septime

3.17 The Remise

- A Step back
- B Step forwards, engage blades in sixte
- A Change engagement to quarte
- B One–two attack with a lunge
- A Parry sixte, counter sixte
- B Return to guard in sixte
- A Disengage riposte with a lunge
- B Parry quarte, disengage riposte
- A Remise and hit

3.18 The Redoublement

1. Engage blades in quarte
    - A Disengage attack in sixte
    - B Parry tierce, don't riposte
    - A Withdraw the arm, attack and hit in seconde

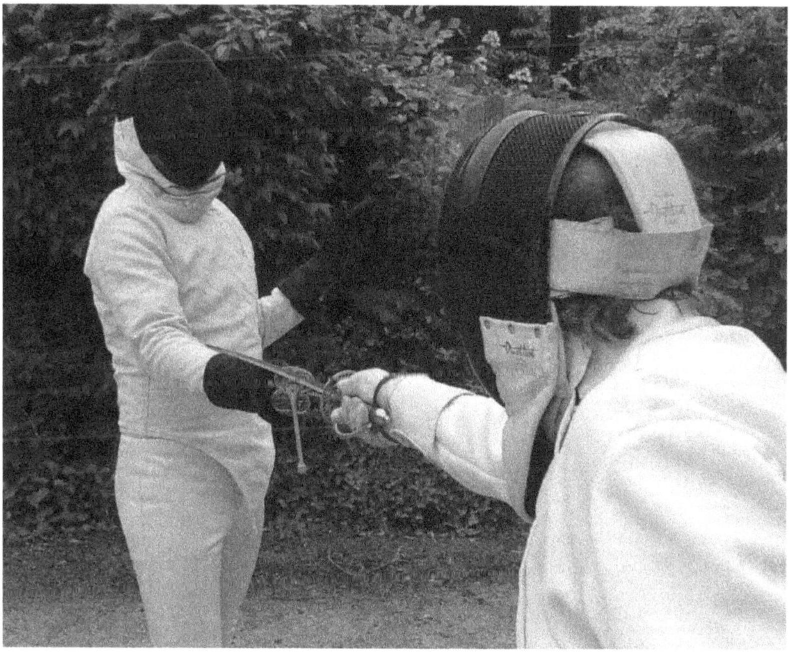

The remise: The fencer on the left has parried quarte and started to disengage without waiting for the attacker to recover, leaving himself open to the remise.

2. Engage blades in tierce
   - A Disengage attack in quarte
   - B Parry quarte, don't riposte
   - A Withdraw the arm, attack and hit in septime
3. Engage blades in quarte
   - A Disengage attack in tierce
   - B Parry septime, don't riposte
   - A Withdraw the arm disengage over the blade, attack and hit in octave
4. Engage blades in tierce
   - A Disengage attack in seconde
   - B Parry seconde, don't riposte
   - A Withdraw the arm, disengage over the blade, attack and hit in septime

5. Engage blades in quarte
   - A Disengage attack in septime
   - B Parry septime, don't riposte
   - A Withdraw the arm, disengage over the blade, attack and hit in seconde
6. Engage blades in tierce
   - A Disengage attack in seconde
   - B Parry prime, don't riposte
   - A Withdraw the arm, disengage over the blade, attack and hit in seconde

3.19 The Reprise

1. Reprise to the rear: engage blades in tierce
   - A disengage attack in quarte
   - B Parry quarte, but don't riposte
   - A Return to guard covering in quarte and immediately disengage attack in tierce and hit
2. Reprise forwards: engage blades in quarte
   - A Disengage attack in tierce
   - B Parry counter-quarte and take a step back
   - A Recover to guard covering in quarte by bringing the back foot forwards, then immediately disengage attack in tierce and hit

3.20 The Beat

1. Engage blades in quarte, beat straight thrust (the defender gives way)
2. Engage blades in quarte, beat disengage attack in sixte (the defender closes the line)
3. Engage blades in tierce, beat straight thrust

4. Engage blades in tierce, beat disengage in quarte
5. Engage blades in quarte, disengage beat, straight thrust in tierce
6. Engage blades in quarte, disengage beat, disengage attack in quarte
7. Engage blades in tierce, disengage beat, straight thrust in quarte
8. Engage blades in tierce, disengage beat, disengage attack in tierce
9. Engage blades in quarte, disengage beat, one-two attack in tierce

3.21 The Coulé

1. Engage blades in quarte, coulé and straight thrust
2. Engage blades in quarte, coulé and disengage attack in tierce
3. Engage blades in tierce, coulé and straight thrust
4. Engage blades in tierce, coulé and disengage attack in quarte
5. Engage blades in quarte, coulé and attack in septime
6. Engage blades in tierce, coulé and attack in octave
7. Engage blades in quarte, coulé and doublé attack in sixte, deceiving a counter-quarte parry
8. Engage blades in tierce, coulé and doublé attack in quarte, deceiving a counter-tierce parry
9. Engage blades in quarte, coulé and one-two attack in quarte, deceiving a simple parry of tierce
10. Engage blades in quarte, coulé and one-two attack in septime, deceiving a simple parry of tierce
11. Engage blades in tierce, coulé and one-two attack in octave, deceiving a simple parry of quarte

3.22 The Pass

1. Engage blades in quarte. Disengage into sixte, attack with a pass
2. Engage blades in quarte. Beat, disengage into sixte, attack with a pass
3. Engage blades in quarte. One-two attack. Move the right foot forwards six inches to provoke the tierce parry, attack with a pass

The pass.

4. Engage blades in tierce. One-two attack. Move the right foot forwards six inches to provoke the quarte parry, attack with a pass
5. Engage blades in tierce. Feint attack to head along the blade, disengage attack in seconde with a pass

3.23 The Croisé

This can either be done quickly and forcefully, hoping to disarm the opponent, or more gently to trap the opponent's blade while riposting.

1. Engage blades in tierce
   - **A** Disengage attack in quarte and stay there
   - **B** Parry quarte, croisé and riposte to flank

The croisé against a straight arm in quarte.

2. As with 1 but continue thus:
   - **A** Turn the hand and parry moving over to seconde, and riposte in seconde

3.24 The Bind

1. Bind from quarte to octave. Start with blades engaged in quarte
   - **A** Disengage attack in tierce and stay there
   - **B** Parry counter-quarte, bind to octave keeping the hand at shoulder height, riposte and hit in octave
2. Bind from tierce to septime. Start with blades engaged in tierce
   - **A** Disengage attack in quarte and stay there
   - **B** Parry counter-tierce, bind to septime keeping the hand at shoulder height, riposte and hit in septime
3. Bind from octave to quarte. Start with blades engaged in sixte
   - **A** Disengage attack in octave and stay there
   - **B** Parry octave, bind to quarte, riposte and hit in quarte
4. Bind from septime to sixte. Start with blades engaged in quarte
   - **A** Disengage attack in septime and stay there
   - **B** Parry septime, bind to sixte, riposte and hit in sixte

3.25 The Demi-volte

1. Engage blades in tierce
   - **A** Leave an opening to encourage a tierce thrust
   - **B** Straight thrust in tierce
   - **A** Disengage, demi-volte and thrust in quarte
2. As with 1 but continue thus:
   - **B** Parry quarte, bind to octave, riposte and hit in octave

Bind from sixte to septime.

The demi-volte.

3.26 Parrying and Deceiving Parries

Start with fencer A on guard in sixte and fencer B standing with the sword arm extended, the point of the blade inside A's blade. Then, on a signal from B, A should try to parry B's blade while B tries to deceive the parry. If B is successful, then A will attempt successive parries while B tries to deceive them all. B should keep the blade movements small, manipulating the weapon mainly with the forefinger and thumb, while A should vary the parries to make B's task more difficult. B is not to press home any attack, and A is not to riposte after finding the blade.

Chapter 4
Simple Fight Sequences

These fight sequences are designed for fencing practice at an intermediate stage between working through and perfecting the exercises and free fighting. Here, you have no need to make quick decisions about what to do next, and there is a better chance of retaining the technical exactness of the actions.

The sequences could also be used as the basis for fencing demonstrations, where long periods of exchanges before a hit is made make it more exciting to watch. The sequences all finish with one fencer getting hit. Another option would be to parry the final thrust and carry on with free play. For demonstration purposes, it is best to avoid aiming for the hand or the lower arm.

The way to practise the sequences is to take them stage by stage. Start by trying just the first attack, parry and riposte, but don't parry that riposte. Then add on the next parry and counter-riposte, etc. The first sequence is broken down into stages as an example. The remaining sequences can easily be broken down in the same way.

These are not sword fights where you are trying to give your opponent a hard time. On the contrary, to make the sequences flow, try to make it easy for your opponent to perform the next movement. If it is a counter-parry, for example, keep your blade close to your opponent's blade as you make your thrust, or you would be more likely to provoke a simple parry. Ceding parries into tierce or quarte can only be attempted if the conditions are just right: bear down on your opponent's blade and thrust directly below the wrist to make this parry easy to execute.

Even though you know your next thrust is going to be parried, do not be tempted to pull it short, but try to make a hit and thrust as if you don't know the parry is coming.

The fight sequences are written up in two-column format. Column A lists the actions made by fencer A, and column B are those made by fencer B. I have kept the descriptions brief, so you will need to understand the language of fencing and how the thrusts and parries are to be made. All the sequences begin with the blades engaged, and fencer A then makes the first move, followed by fencer B. Sometimes the action from B has to be synchronised with the action from A rather than following on after it has been completed. Always read ahead, too, because sometimes the next action from fencer A, as shown on the next line down, has to be synchronised with the response from B.

If you can find a third party to read out the movements and check that you are performing them correctly, you will find it a great help.

FIGHT SEQUENCE 1

Engage blades in tierce

	A	B
(a)	Press on the blade and close the line	Disengage attack in quarte and hit
(b)	Press on the blade and close the line	Disengage attack in quarte
	Parry counter-tierce	Recover to tierce
	Disengage riposte in quarte and hit	

	A	B
(c)	Press on the blade and close the line	Disengage attack in quarte
	Parry counter-tierce	Recover to tierce
	Disengage riposte in quarte	Parry quarte, direct riposte in quarte and hit
(d)	Press on the blade and close the line	Disengage attack in quarte
	Parry counter-tierce	Recover to tierce
	Disengage riposte in quarte	Parry quarte, direct riposte in quarte
	Parry quarte	Recover to quarte
	One–two riposte and hit	Parry tierce on the feint (deceived)
(e)	Press on the blade and close the line	Disengage attack in quarte
	Parry counter-tierce	Recover to tierce
	Disengage riposte in quarte	Parry quarte, direct riposte in quarte
	Parry quarte	Recover to quarte

	A	B
	One–two riposte	Parry tierce, counter-tierce, riposte in octave and hit
(f)	Press on the blade and close the line	Disengage attack in quarte
	Parry counter-tierce	Recover to tierce
	Disengage riposte in quarte	Parry quarte, direct riposte in quarte
	Parry quarte	Recover to quarte
	One–two riposte	Parry tierce, counter-tierce, riposte in octave
	Parry octave	Recover to octave
	Disengage riposte in septime and hit	
(g)	Press on the blade and close the line	Disengage attack in quarte
	Parry counter-tierce	Recover to tierce
	Disengage riposte in quarte	Parry quarte, direct riposte in quarte
	Parry quarte	Recover to quarte

A	B
One–two riposte	Parry tierce, counter-tierce, riposte in octave
Parry octave	Recover to octave
Disengage riposte in septime	Parry counter-octave
Recover to octave	Riposte in tierce and hit

FIGHT SEQUENCE 2

Engage blades in quarte

A	B
Press on the blade and close the line	Disengage attack in tierce
Parry septime, riposte in septime	Parry septime
Recover to septime	Indirect riposte in octave
Parry counter-septime, riposte in quarte	Parry quarte
Recover to quarte	Doublé riposte in quarte
Parry counter-quarte, tierce	Recover to tierce
One–two attack in tierce	Parry quarte, tierce

A	B
Recover to tierce	Doublé riposte in quarte
Counter-tierce twice, forced riposte in tierce	Parry prime, flying cut-over, riposte, and hit in quarte

FIGHT SEQUENCE 3

Engage blades in tierce

A	B
Step forwards, changing to quarte	Step back and move to quarte
Step forwards, changing to tierce	Counter-disengage and straighten the arm
Parry counter-tierce	Recover to tierce
One–two attack in tierce	Parry quarte counter-quarte, riposte in quarte
Parry quarte, riposte in quarte	Parry quarte
Recover to quarte	Indirect riposte in tierce
Step back, parry septime	Reprise forwards, riposte in octave
Parry counter-septime	Recover to septime
Feint to quarte, riposte in septime	Parry quarte, septime, bind to sixte, riposte in sixte

A	B
Ceding parry into tierce	Recover to sixte
Doublé riposte in quarte and hit	Parry counter sixte, which is deceived

FIGHT SEQUENCE 4

Engage blades in tierce

A	B
Step back changing to quarte	Step forwards covering in quarte
Step back changing to tierce	Step forwards covering in tierce
Step back changing to quarte	Step forwards, counter-disengage riposte in tierce
Parry counter-quarte, direct riposte	Parry quarte, direct riposte
Parry quarte	Recover to quarte
Recover to tierce	Doublé attack in quarte
Parry counter-tierce, octave, direct riposte	Ceding parry to quarte
Recover to quarte	Step back
Step forwards, beat direct attack in quarte	Demi-volte and hit in quarte

FIGHT SEQUENCE 5

Engage blades in quarte

A	B
Beat disengage attack in tierce	Cover in quarte, parry tierce
Recover to tierce	Cut-over disengage riposte in tierce
Parry quarte, counter-quarte, riposte in quarte	Parry quarte, riposte in quarte
Parry quarte, riposte in quarte	Parry quarte
Recover to quarte, step back	Step forwards, disengage riposte in tierce
Step back, parry tierce	Reprise forwards, disengage riposte in quarte
Parry quarte	Recover to quarte
Disengage riposte in tierce with a pass	Parry tierce, forced riposte in tierce
Take left leg back and parry prime, riposte in prime	Parry prime, sidestep right, riposte in seconde
Parry septime, riposte in septime	Parry septime, riposte in quarte
Parry quarte, deflect the blade with the left hand, riposte in quarte and hit	

FIGHT SEQUENCE 6

This one is the most complex of the set, but it comprises three short sequences joined together, which can be learned separately. The third part starts in quarte and ends with a hit. Learn this part first. The second part starts in octave and ends in quarte. Learn this one next and then try going through the second and third parts without a break. Finally, practise the first sequence, which starts in tierce and ends in octave, and then see if you can run through all three parts. Note that fencers can switch between being A and B for each part if desired.

Part 1: Engage blades in tierce

A	B
Step forwards with pressure on the blade	Step back covering in tierce
Disengage attack in quarte	Parry counter-tierce, direct riposte
Parry septime, riposte in septime	Parry septime
Recover to septime	Step forwards with a change to octave
Step back cover in octave	

Part 2: Engage blades in octave

A	B
	Attack in tierce
Parry tierce, riposte in seconde	Parry seconde

A	B
Recover to seconde	Feint to tierce, riposte to seconde
Parry tierce, seconde	Recover to seconde
One-two: feint to tierce, riposte in quarte	Parry tierce, quarte
Recover to quarte, step back	Step forwards

Part 3: Engage blades in quarte

A	B
	Beat, one-two attack in quarte
On the beat, close the line in quarte, parry tierce, counter-tierce, forced direct riposte	Return to guard parrying prime, sidestep to the right, riposte in seconde
Recover to prime, bind to sixte, and indirect riposte in quarte	Cover in sixte, parry quarte, riposte in quarte
Recover with a change of engagement and parry sixte	Recover to sixte
Indirect riposte to quarte	Parry counter sixte, indirect riposte in quarte
Parry counter sixte, double riposte to quarte and hit	Parry counter sixte

Chapter 5

Learning to Feel

When swords are engaged, both fencers can enjoy a moment of relative safety, secure in the knowledge that only a small movement is needed to close the line in the event of a direct attack being attempted, and knowing for certain that one area will not be attacked if the opponent disengages. The exercises in this chapter all start with blades crossed, then one fencer performs an action that the other, with eyes closed, must feel through the blade and react in a pre-determined way.

One fencer is to play the part of the instructor while the other, with eyes shut, plays the pupil. In all cases, the instructor explains what to do, then the eyes are shut, they both run through the exercise and the eyes can be opened again. The instructor must comment on whether the exercise was carried out correctly or not, and if not, it should be repeated until it is performed successfully. It is a good idea to try the exercises with the eyes open first, so both fencers know exactly what to do.

5.1 Straight Thrust

1. Engage blades in tierce, close the eyes The instructor closes the line in tierce
   The pupil disengages and attacks with a lunge in quarte
2. As with 1, but engage and close the line in quarte, and attack into tierce

5.2 Counter-disengage Attack

1. Engage blades in tierce, close the eyes
   The instructor changes engagement to quarte
   The pupil counter-disengages into tierce, avoiding blade contact, lunges and hits
2. As with 1, but engage blades in quarte, the instructor changes to tierce and the pupil counter-disengage into quarte

5.3 Parrying a Disengage Attack or a One–Two Attack, Followed by a Direct Riposte

1. Engage blades in tierce, close the eyes
   The instructor has a choice of a simple attack or a one–two attack. On completion, stay on the lunge
   The pupil is to take a simple parry of quarte, and if the blade is found, riposte, otherwise take a counter-quarte parry and riposte. The riposte is to be made by straightening the arm without lunging
2. As 1, but engage blades in quarte. The pupil takes a simple parry of tierce, and then counter-tierce if the blade is not found

5.4 Parrying a Disengage Attack or a Doublé Attack, Followed by an Indirect Riposte

1. Engage blades in tierce, close the eyes
   The instructor has a choice of a simple attack or doublé attack, followed by recovering to guard in tierce keeping blade contact

The pupil takes a counter-tierce parry and, if the blade is found, disengages and ripostes with a lunge as the instructor's blade is withdrawn. If the blade is not found, the pupil takes a second counter-parry followed by a disengage riposte

2. As 1, but engage blades in quarte, the pupil to take one or two counter-quarte parries.
3. Engage blades in sixte

   Same idea as above, but the instructor has the choice of a simple attack into octave, or to deceive the pupil's octave parry by disengaging over the blade and attacking in septime

   The pupil is to parry octave and, if the blade is not found, a further counter-octave parry. As the instructor recovers to guard in octave keeping blade contact, the pupil disengages and ripostes with a lunge in septime
4. As 1, but engage blades in quarte, the feint/attack to be made in septime, and the pupil to parry septime and counter-septime if necessary. As the instructor returns to septime, the pupil's disengage riposte will be in octave

5.5 Ceding Parries

These parries can only be taken if the conditions are favourable, so it's important to get the exercises working successfully with the eyes open first.

1. Engage blades in sixte, the pupil's arm extended with the blade horizontal. The instructor takes a bind from sixte to septime and straightens his arm. The pupil takes a ceding parry into tierce, followed by a direct riposte
2. Engage blades in quarte, the pupil's arm extended with the blade horizontal. The instructor rakes a bind from quarte to octave and straightens his arm. The pupil takes a ceding parry into quarte, followed by a direct riposte

3. Engage blades in tierce. The master forces over the blade aiming above the wrist, and closing the distance. The pupil takes a prime parry and ripostes in prime without lunging

5.6 *Prises de Fer* (Taking the Blade)

1. The envelopment
   Engage blades in sixte. Close the eyes
   The instructor straightens the arm with a coulé along the blade and steps close enough for the pupil to hit without lunging
   The pupil executes an envelopment, straightens the arm and hits
2. Bind from sixte to septime
   As 1, but the pupil executes a bind into septime and ripostes in septime
3. Bind from quarte to octave
   As 1, but start with blades engaged in quarte; the pupil binds into octave and ripostes in octave
4. The croisé
   Engage blades in quarte. Close the eyes
   The instructor straightens the arm with a coulé along the blade and steps close enough for the pupil to hit without lunging.
   The pupil executes a croisé and ripostes

Chapter 6

Some Sparring Tips

6.1 General Advice

Do

- Remember the main objective is to avoid getting hit. With this weapon you don't want to hit your opponent before he hits you as they do in competitive fencing – you don't want to get hit at all. It may help if you try to imagine that the swords are sharp.
- Look for opportunities to practise all the moves you learned when working through the exercises.
- Always acknowledge hits against you. To be valid, hits must have character of penetration – mere touches that would do no damage if the weapons were sharp do not count. Own up if your opponent acknowledges a hit but you don't believe it was good enough.
- Develop a good defence by practising all the parries rather than relying on the more instinctive simple ones all the time. Concentrate on your weaker parries until they become second nature. If you are weaker defending yourself in quarte, say, then spend more time coming on guard in quarte. Ensure that every parry arrives precisely in one of the recognised guard positions.
- When attacking, remember the basic principles: always start with a straight arm, with the hand above the shoulder, then lunge and cover into the opposing blade to protect yourself from the sword point. Push off from the rear of the back foot when lunging and keep the foot flat on the ground.
- Try to fence with blade contact if your opponent will accept it so you can feel as well as see every blade movement.

- To encourage more interesting swordplay, try a bout where only hits with the riposte count and hits on the initial attack are ignored.
- Avoid double hits at all costs. Parrying is much safer than launching a counter-attack. Do not attempt a time-hit unless you are sure you can close the line of the attack, or a stop-hit unless you are certain it will prevent the attack from arriving.
- If you are a novice, it is better to partner an experienced fencer who is likely to respond in the correct way and execute the moves well.
- If you are an experienced fencer partnering a novice, be sure to stick to the rules of fencing and allow hits to be scored against you provided the fencing is correct.
- Be aware of how exposed your sword hand is – the shell guards on smallswords do not offer much protection.
- Be very wary of getting too close to your opponent as there is always a risk that your blade could be grabbed.
- Try to beat your opponent with fencing skill rather than speed. As an exercise, it can be useful to fence deliberately slowly to encourage more blade exchanges and more compound attacks and ripostes, rather like the way one might fence with a beginner.
- Try making some feints to see if your opponent reacts in a predictable way – you may then be able to plan a compound attack.

Don't

- If you are new to fencing, do not try sparring until you have mastered the exercises under supervision and practised the fight sequences.
- Do not be obsessed with counting the hits – the only one that matters is the next one. The quality of the fencing is more important than the score.
- Do not always expect to score a hit with a simple attack; explore other possibilities – plan to hit on a riposte or counter-riposte rather than the initial attack. Try leaving a part of your target exposed to entice an attack that you can easily parry and follow with a riposte.

- Do not launch fast violent attacks that leave you unable to deal with a riposte if the attack is parried.
- Never allow hilts to collide – this is fighting rather than fencing, and the jolt can injure the opponent's hand or wrist.
- When you are close enough to land a hit without lunging, never jab – just straighten the arm enough to reach and place the point on the target.
- Do not be predictable by always repeating the same actions.
- Do not stop as soon as your attack is parried or as soon as you have parried an attack. Try to keep a sequence of thrusts and parries going for as long as you can until one of you scores a hit.
- When an attack fails, do not remain on the lunge repeatedly jabbing away with renewed attacks, but return to guard quickly while remaining ready to parry a riposte.

6.2 The Flècher

Flèche attacks (instead of lunging, the attacker runs past, hoping to land a hit on the way) are not usually encountered in smallsword fencing, but you may have to defend yourself against them. If the opponent hasn't dislodged your blade before launching the attack, then a time-hit may be possible. If your blade has been beaten down, then a rapid demi-volte combined with a prime parry could be a useful defence. Note that the fight does not stop if the attacker runs past, which gives you a considerable advantage if the attack fails.

6.3 The Counter-attacker

Some sports fencing opponents will respond to every attack with a counter-attack instead of attempting a parry. While this is risky in smallsword fencing, opponents with a longer reach than you are particularly menacing, and they may be able to hit and prevent your attack from arriving. *Counter-time* is the best strategy to use against these stop-hitters. Do not commit yourself to an attack, but do just enough to provoke the counter-attack, which you can then parry and follow with a riposte. This is not quite as easy as it sounds because you can't risk a riposte with detachment – this opponent will not be interested in parrying it but will seek to press home his counter-attack. It may be necessary to bind the blade after the parry to get into a good position for riposting along the blade.

6.4 Opponents Who Prefer Absence of Blade

You will almost certainly meet opponents who abhor making blade contact, as this has become the norm in modern sports fencing. Most fencers will immediately disengage as soon as you make blade contact. This disengagement itself may provide an opening for a counter-disengage attack. Clearly attacks cannot start with a disengagement when the blades are already disengaged, which makes standard one–two and doublé attacks impossible. A useful approach is to try some straight thrust feints and some beats on the blade to determine the likely response before following through and deceiving the predicted parry. You will be much more successful with compound attacks if you are able to deceive parries while you are on the lunge, which is why it is so important to spend time developing the skills before starting fighting.

While attacks will need to be a bit different with this opponent, ripostes can be made as usual, as the blades are always engaged again once a parry has been successful and conditions will be right for a one–two or doublé riposte, depending on how the opponent chooses to parry.

6.5 Opponents Who Can't Fence

These can be tricky opponents to deal with because their actions are not derived from standard fencing theory, making them unfamiliar and unpredictable. They are good fighters and generally fast, too, but normally they have weaknesses that can be exploited, for example:

- Don't worry about being hit with a compound attack or riposte because these opponents won't be attempting anything that complicated.
- They are unlikely to try a circular parry, so there will probably be no opportunity for a doublé attack or riposte.
- Their simple parries, if they can be credited with that description, will be wild and uncontrolled. If they carry the hand across laterally as they should, they will likely displace the point much further. This creates a good opportunity for a one-two attack, and if they don't find your feint, they will be surprised because it is the blade contact that terminates the parry. Hence if you manage to deceive the parry, they will overshoot, making it much harder for them to move back in the opposite direction to parry the main attack – simple parries followed by counter-parries are unlikely to be in their repertoire. If they move the hand diagonally downwards when parrying, be ready immediately to move your point down and round the hilt, trying not to make blade contact.
- Attacking with a feint in octave or seconde will often reveal another weakness in their defence. They will likely try to smash downwards on your blade, giving you a good opportunity to deceive this wild movement and attack in sixte or tierce. They will probably hit the floor with the point before they realise the parry has failed.
- If these fencers seem amenable to being corrected, you may be able to set them on the path to learning how to fence properly.

6.6 Scoring Ideas

When counting hits, it is important to ensure that nobody gains from a double hit. While this could identify a winner in a sports competition, it would spell the end for both duellists in a real sword fight, and we want to make smallsword fencing more like the combat situation. For those who are concerned to know who is winning, a few ideas for scoring are outlined here:

The Duelling Survivor

This can be fun at the end of an evening with a few friends. The idea is to see which of the group would survive if you were fighting with real swords. Pair off and have a fight for one hit. The one who is hit in each pair is then knocked out, and the survivors pair off again and the process is repeated until only one fencer remains. In the event of a double hit, both fencers are knocked out, so if this happens when starting with only three fencers, the winner is the one who doesn't have to fight.

Multiple Duels

Here, everyone fights everyone else for one hit as described above, and the number of defeats for each fencer are compared – the one with the fewest being the winner. This may result in a tie, which could be resolved with another fight for one hit.

The Tennis Score

This scoring works rather like a tennis match starting from deuce. The first fencer to hit gains a point. If he lands the next hit, he is the winner, but if the other fencer hits next or if there is a double hit, the scores revert to zero. A limit can be placed on the number of double hits allowed in a bout – both fencers could be knocked out after three double hits, for example.

First to Three

The first fencer to receive three hits is knocked out, but a double hit clears both scores to zero. After three double hits, both fencers are knocked out.

Body and Limbs

Hits on the head or torso count as two points, while hits on the limbs count as one point. Double hits anywhere reset the scores to zero, and three double hits result in a loss for both fencers. The winner could be the first to score five hits, or whatever is convenient.

The Ladder

This is fun for a larger group of fencers. It needs an even number of at least half a dozen fencers. Form two ranks facing each other. Each pair of fencers represents a rung of the ladder. Decide which end is the bottom rung and which is the top. If some fencers are known to be stronger, start them on the lower rungs. Each pair then fights to determine a winner. On the bottom rung, the loser stays put, while on the top rung, the winner stays put. In all other cases, the winner moves up a rung, and the loser moves down a rung. The procedure is then repeated at least as many times as the number of rungs on the ladder, and this process will shunt the stronger fencers towards the top of the ladder and the weaker ones towards the lower rungs. The close proximity of pairs will obviously restrict the normal sideways movements that are allowed in smallsword fencing.

Conclusion

With their well-documented school of fencing, the eighteenth-century French masters succeeded in turning swordplay into an art that was initially of invaluable use for self-defence and duelling and later enjoyed as recreation. It has been said that art is not a competition, and the modern pressures to turn fencing into a competitive sport have seen to it that the art, as conceived by the early fencing masters, has now been almost entirely lost. Sporting bodies are not good custodians of swordsmanship because their interest is entirely in competition successes, and the sport bears little resemblance to the duelling for which the art evolved. Swordplay is now generally rather pedestrian, with hits being scored without much fencing taking place. There is more fencing to be seen in HEMA clubs than in sports fencing clubs.

For those who are interested in the fencing itself, as opposed to just using simple movements to score points, and who are prepared to spend time learning the skills, the smallsword is an excellent weapon to choose. It closely resembles the swords that were used for duelling in the eighteenth century. It is light and easy to handle, and fights with this weapon will be more like the real thing. The fact that the left hand can be used and that fencers are not restricted to a piste adds variety and interest to the fencing. There is no real reason why it should not feature more often as a weapon of choice in sports clubs. It is reasonably straightforward for foilists to transition to the smallsword, but not so easy for épéeists because they are too keen on launching counter-attacks instead of parrying, and this inevitably results in more double hits, which are bad news in smallsword fencing.

The exercises set down here have a good provenance. Most of them are derived from French fencing manuals published over 250 years ago. They are not out of date, however, and will be familiar to anyone who has been taught foil in the French classical manner. Practising and perfecting the exercises will be time well spent. After these have been mastered, some self-discipline will be needed when sparring to ensure that all the thrusts and parries are executed correctly.

How long does it take to master the smallsword? J. D. Aylward, referring to the years following the French revolution, made this interesting comment in *The Small-Sword in England*:

> **... while the French have always taken the arts seriously, and in the case of the sword believed that three years' unremitting practice was required before a man could call himself a swordsman, the English amateurs thought that three months was more than sufficient to devote to what they regarded more as a healthy exercise than as a vital means of defence.**

There is a lot to learn, and it takes time to learn to fence well. Realistically, fencing once a week, beginners will need about a year's drilling before trying their hand at sparring, otherwise their attempts will likely be a complete scrap, unrelated to fencing. Those who are impatient to start fighting before they know anything, or who are overly concerned about scoring hits, would be best advised to stick with sports fencing, where this way of working is tolerated. Without practising and mastering all the fencing skills, the smallsword will offer no advantages. When I started fencing, I was told it usually took seven years to become an accomplished fencer.

If you have no option but to start out with sports fencing, you might care to refer to Roger Crosnier's *Fencing with the Foil*, which covers all the classical theory. In his day, foil fencing hadn't diverged very far from how it was taught as a practice weapon for the smallsword, so it is a good stepping stone towards smallsword fencing. I don't know how much theory modern coaches are required to know, but we do know that

French classical fencing as such is no longer taught in sports fencing clubs, and the evidence certainly suggests that modern students are not well versed in the theory and language of fencing. Masters who are weak on theory have been around for a long time - in 1771, Jean Olivier made this comment:

Nothing is more common than to see masters who from long practice fence well, and who depending solely on their reputation in that particular, neglect and are ignorant of the most essential part of their business.

If both opponents in a bout have learned to fence in the same traditional manner and are able to keep longer fight sequences going, the bout will always be enjoyable: the fun of fencing lies in the intricacies of the thrusts and parries exchanged before a hit is landed. The short fight sequences included in this book give a flavour of the sort of exchanges that can be made.

I hope this book will help everyone to become better fencers, enjoy practising and sparring with the smallsword and, more importantly, play a part in keeping the art of swordsmanship alive.

Reading List

The Small Sword in England; J. D. Aylward; Hutchinson of London; 1960

Fencing with the Foil; Roger Crosnier; Faber & Faber; 1961

Fencing Familiarized; Jean Olivier; John Bell, London; 1771

Theory and Practice of Fencing; J. McArthur; 1780 Facsimile from The Naval & Military Press Ltd

The School of Fencing; Domenico Angelo; 1787; Facsimile from Frontline Books

The Art of the Smallsword; P. J. F. Girard; 1740; Translation by Philip Crawley; Wyvern Media Ltd; 2014

Edged Weapons; Frederick Wilkinson; Guinness Signatures; 1970

The Swordsman; Alfred Hutton; 1890s; Facsimile from The Naval and Military Press Ltd.

The Boy's Modern Playmate; Rev J. G. Wood, editor; Frederick Warne & Co.; 1890

About the Author

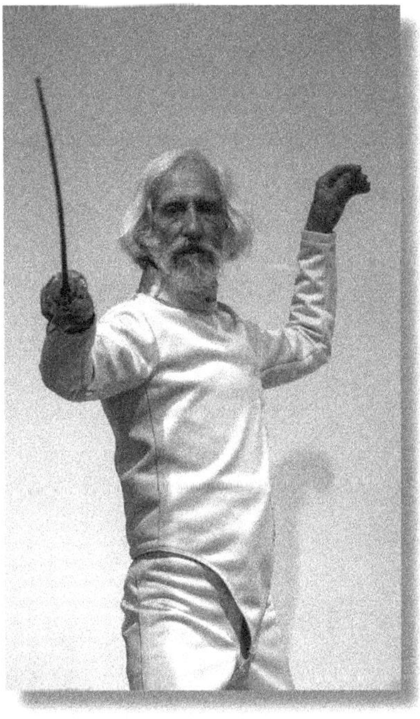

Michael Stevens started fencing as a college student in the late 1960s. In those days the teaching, now referred to as 'classical', had not changed significantly from how it was done two centuries earlier. Michael practised fencing with foil, sabre and épée, gained a reputation for adopting a classical style, and assisted with teaching novices. He continued fencing regularly through his working life as a computer scientist at a metrology laboratory and into retirement.

Growing disappointment with the way modern competitive fencing has diverged from its origins led to his recent interest in smallsword fencing, which better captures the spirit of duelling and where all the old fencing theories still apply.

Michael's other interests include horse riding, and he enjoys working on the potter's wheel and specialises in porcelain. He has previously published books on schooling horses and pottery. Michael currently resides in England.

Credits

Cover and interior design:	Anja Elsen
Layout:	DiTech Publishing Services, www.ditechpubs.com
Cover photo:	© AdobeStock; Barbara Stevens
Interior photos:	Courtesy of Michael Stevens, may not be used without publisher permission
Managing editor:	Elizabeth Evans
Copy editor:	Sarah Tomblin, www.sarahtomblinediting.com